The World's Greatest Unsolved Mysteries

Echoes of the Unexplained

Graham Hodson

Contents

Introduction

Welcome to a world veiled in shadows, a journey through the corridors of the unknown. "The World's Greatest Unsolved Mysteries: Echoes of the Unexplained" is not just a book, it's an odyssey into the uncharted territories of human curiosity and wonder.

In these pages, you will find a collection of stories that have mystified, intrigued, and sometimes even terrified people across generations and geographies. From the enigmatic depths of the ocean to the far reaches of outer space, from ancient riddles left by lost civilizations to modern-day enigmas that challenge our understanding of the world, this book covers a wide spectrum of mysteries that remain unsolved to this day.

Each story is a puzzle, a question mark in the vast expanse of human knowledge. We delve into legends like the Bermuda Triangle, where ships and planes disappear without a trace. We explore the cryptic symbols of the Voynich Manuscript, a book written in an unknown language with illustrations that baffle the brightest of minds. We question the origins of the mysterious Nazca Lines, vast geoglyphs etched into the Peruvian desert, visible only from the sky.

But it's not just about places or ancient artefacts. We also bring you tales of unexplained phenomena, eerie accounts of ghost ships sailing the seas, and the perplexing case of individuals who vanished into thin air. Each story is a piece of the puzzle, a fragment of the larger mystery that is our existence.

"The World's Greatest Unsolved Mysteries" is more than a compilation of the unexplained; it's an invitation to wonder, to question, and to imagine. It's a tribute to the unquenchable human spirit that constantly seeks answers, the spirit that makes us look up at the stars and dream, and the spirit that refuses to accept the mundane as the only reality.

As you turn these pages, we invite you to open your mind to the possibilities. Some stories might send a chill down your spine, some might make you ponder deeply, and others might inspire you to seek answers of your own. In the end, each story, each mystery, is a reminder that the world is far more complex and fascinating than we often realize.

So, embark on this journey with us. Explore the unknown. Delve into the tales of "The World's Greatest Unsolved Mysteries" and let your imagination soar into the realms of the unexplained with fascinating mysteries from around the world that remain... unsolved.

The Disappearance of Amelia Earhart: A Flight into Mystery

The tale of Amelia Earhart's disappearance is not just a story of a vanished aviator; it's a narrative that encapsulates the spirit of an era, the allure of the unknown, and the enduring intrigue of an unsolved mystery. Amelia Earhart, a name synonymous with adventure and bravery, vanished over the Pacific Ocean in 1937 during her audacious attempt to circumnavigate the globe. Her disappearance remains one of the most compelling enigmas of the 20th century.

Amelia Earhart was more than a pioneering aviator; she was a symbol of the new frontiers opening for women in the early 20th century. With her leather jacket, tousled hair, and a smile that spoke of an unquenchable zest for life, she captured the imagination of the world. Her accomplishments in aviation were not just records; they were declarations of a bold, new spirit of independence and daring.

The final flight, which would seal her place in the annals of mystery, began with ambition and hope. Along with her navigator, Fred Noonan, Earhart embarked on a 29,000-mile journey, a flight that would make her the first woman to fly around the world along the equator. Her twin-engine Lockheed Electra took off from Miami on June 1, 1937, and the journey proceeded through South America, Africa, India, and Southeast Asia, arriving in New Guinea on June 29th. Only 7,000 miles remained of her momentous journey.

The next leg of the flight was to be a challenging one: a 2,556-mile trek across the vast Pacific Ocean to Howland Island, a tiny sliver of land barely visible on the map. It was during this leg, on July 2nd, that Earhart and Noonan lost radio contact. The last words received from Earhart were a chilling testament to her predicament: "We are on the line 157 337... We are running north and south."

An extensive search ensued, led by the United States Navy and Coast Guard, covering over 250,000 square miles of ocean. Despite these efforts, neither Earhart, Noonan, nor the Electra were ever found. The disappearance sparked a flurry of theories: Did they crash into the ocean after running out of fuel? Were they captured by the Japanese, as some conspiracy theories suggest? Or did they manage to land on an uninhabited island, only to eventually succumb to the elements?

Over the decades, numerous expeditions have attempted to find clues to Earhart's fate. Some have claimed to find fragments of her plane or personal effects on remote Pacific islands, fueling speculation but providing no definitive answers. The mystery of Amelia Earhart's disappearance continues to fascinate, a symbol of human ambition and the unyielding allure of the unknown.

Graham Hodson

Jack the Ripper: The Elusive Shadow in the Fog

In the darkened, fog-laden alleys of Victorian London, a sinister figure lurks, a specter whose name would become synonymous with terror: Jack the Ripper. The identity of this infamous and unidentified serial killer, who haunted the Whitechapel district in the late 19th century, remains one of the most enduring and chilling mysteries in the annals of crime.

The year is 1888. The East End of London is a place of stark contrasts: a bustling hub of industry and poverty, of crowded living and hidden vices. It's in this shadowy backdrop that Jack the Ripper emerged, preying on the most vulnerable—women who eked out a meager living in the gas-lit streets.

The Ripper's reign of terror is marked by a series of brutal murders. The victims, all women, were not just killed; they were mutilated with a savagery that suggested a deep rage and a disturbingly clinical interest in the human anatomy. The canonical five—Mary Ann Nichols, Annie Chapman, Elizabeth Stride, Catherine Eddowes, and Mary Jane Kelly—were left in the open, their bodies a gruesome tableau that spoke of a killer both brazen and calculating.

The Ripper's methods were horrifyingly consistent: throat slashed, abdomen mutilated, organs sometimes removed.

The sheer brutality of the killings, coupled with the Ripper's ability to evade capture, sowed seeds of fear and paranoia across London. Newspapers fed on the terror, sensationalizing the murders and even receiving taunting letters purportedly from the killer, giving rise to the name "Jack the Ripper."

The police investigation, hampered by limited forensic technology and plagued by public and media pressure, yielded more questions than answers. Over 2,000 people were interviewed, and hundreds were investigated, yet the Ripper's identity remained elusive. Theories about who he could have been abound, ranging from a butcher or a physician to a member of the royal family. However, the lack of definitive evidence has turned each hypothesis into mere conjecture.

The Ripper's identity is not just a question of a name; it's a puzzle that delves into the heart of human darkness. The murders stopped as suddenly as they had started, leaving behind a legacy that continues to fascinate and horrify. The Ripper was never caught, never unmasked, and thus, he remains a ghost in the annals of crime, a cipher for the ultimate unsolvable mystery.

Jack the Ripper's story is more than a tale of murder; it's a narrative that reflects the societal, cultural, and technological limitations of the time. The enigma of his identity is a dark mirror held up to the era he stalked, a reminder of the perpetual struggle between lawlessness and justice. The shadow of Jack the Ripper looms large, a chilling reminder of the abyss that lies in the unknown.

The Voynich Manuscript: A Medieval Mystery

Aspects of the Voynich Manuscript's tale seem like they could seamlessly integrate into a Dan Brown novel. This enigmatic, age-old manuscript, 234 pages in length, is composed in an unknown language, a puzzle that has baffled experts and cryptanalysts for generations.

In the pantheon of historical mysteries, few artifacts are as captivating or as confounding as the Voynich Manuscript. This medieval tome, filled with pages of an unknown language and cryptic illustrations, has baffled linguists, cryptographers, and historians alike for centuries. It's a puzzle written in ink, a riddle wrapped in vellum.

The Voynich Manuscript, named after the Polish-American bookseller Wilfrid Voynich, who acquired it in 1912, is believed to have been composed in the 15th century, based on carbon dating of the vellum. The book's origins, authorship, and purpose remain shrouded in mystery. Its pages are filled with what appears to be a unique alphabet, completely unlike any known writing system. The text flows in smooth, rhythmic patterns, suggesting it holds meaning, yet this meaning has eluded decipherment.

Adding to the enigma are the illustrations that adorn its pages. These drawings range from the seemingly mundane to the outright bizarre. There are botanical illustrations of plants that do not match any known species, astronomical diagrams depicting unknown constellations, and biological drawings of tiny, naked people in strange, interconnected tubular structures. There are also pages of what appear to be pharmaceutical recipes, with unrecognizable herbal concoctions.

The manuscript's language, often called "Voynichese," has been the subject of intense study and speculation. It has been analyzed by some of the best minds in cryptology, including those who cracked the Enigma code in World War II. Yet, it defies classification. Its alphabet has around 20 to 25 distinct characters, but there is no obvious punctuation. The structure of the words and sentences suggests a natural language, but it bears no relation to any European or Asian tongue.

Many theories have been proposed about the manuscript's purpose and origins. Some suggest it's a pharmacopeia, an elaborate medical text. Others believe it may be an alchemical manuscript or a treatise on medieval science. More exotic theories propose that it's a document from another world or dimension, or a hoax, a linguistic puzzle designed to confound.

The Voynich Manuscript has also been subjected to numerous attempts at decipherment, with claims of breakthroughs that have often led to dead ends or controversy. The mystery is compounded by the possibility that the manuscript could be a sophisticated hoax, although the expertise and knowledge required to create such a work in the 15th century would be remarkable in itself.

Today, the Voynich Manuscript resides in the Beinecke Rare Book & Manuscript Library at Yale University, tantalizing and mysterious as ever. It remains an enigma, a challenge to our understanding of history, language, and the human penchant for puzzles. Its pages are a silent testament to the unknown, a reminder that there are still mysteries waiting to be unraveled in the shadows of the past.

Graham Hodson

The Bermuda Triangle: A Mysterious Maritime Enigma

In the vast expanse of the North Atlantic Ocean, there lies a realm shrouded in mystery and fear, a place where the known laws of physics and explanations of science seem to falter. This is the Bermuda Triangle, an enigmatic stretch of ocean bounded by Miami, Bermuda, and Puerto Rico. Over the years, it has become synonymous with the unexplained, a maritime black hole where ships and airplanes have vanished under circumstances that defy rational explanation.

The story of the Bermuda Triangle is a tapestry woven from tales of lost vessels and ghost ships, of planes disappearing off the radar, never to be seen again. The legend began to take shape in the 20th century, with a series of disappearances that captured the public's imagination. One of the most famous incidents was the disappearance of Flight 19 in 1945, a training flight of five TBM Avenger bombers that vanished without a trace. The flight leader's last transmission, "We are entering white water, nothing seems right," only deepened the aura of mystery.

As the lore of the Bermuda Triangle grew, so did the list of unexplained disappearances. The USS Cyclops, a massive Navy cargo ship, disappeared in 1918 with 306 crew and passengers, leaving no trace. The civilian freighter SS Cotopaxi vanished in 1925, only to become a ghost ship in maritime legends. Aircraft, too, seemed to fall victim to the

Triangle's curse, with notable disappearances including the Star Tiger in 1948 and the Star Ariel in 1949.

Theories attempting to explain these mysteries are as diverse as they are imaginative. Some propose natural explanations like rogue waves, methane hydrates erupting from the ocean floor, or unpredictable weather patterns. Others veer into the realm of the fantastical, suggesting magnetic anomalies, underwater alien bases, or even a portal to another dimension.

Despite the allure of such theories, skeptics argue that the Bermuda Triangle is no more mysterious than any other part of the ocean. They point out that the region is heavily traveled, and when you factor in human error, mechanical failure, and natural disasters, the number of incidents doesn't seem so extraordinary. Moreover, investigations have demystified some of the incidents, attributing them to navigational errors or bad weather.

Yet, the Bermuda Triangle continues to captivate the collective imagination. It's a symbol of the unknown, a metaphor for the unexplored and unexplained mysteries of our planet. Each story, each disappearance, is a puzzle piece in an enigmatic mosaic. The Bermuda Triangle challenges our understanding of the natural world and reminds us that, despite our advancements, there are still mysteries out there, lurking in the deep, waiting to be unraveled.

The Dyatlov Pass Incident: A Mystery in the Snow

In the cold winter of 1959, a chilling event unfolded in the Ural Mountains of the Soviet Union, which would later be known as the Dyatlov Pass Incident. This mysterious case involves the unexplained deaths of nine experienced hikers and has baffled investigators, researchers, and enthusiasts for decades. The bizarre circumstances surrounding their demise have spawned countless theories, ranging from the plausible to the outlandish, yet the truth remains elusive.

The story began in January 1959 when a group of young hikers, most of them students or graduates from the Ural Polytechnical Institute, embarked on a skiing expedition across the northern Ural Mountains. Led by Igor Dyatlov, for whom the pass was later named, the team consisted of eight men and two women. They were all skilled mountaineers and had experience in long ski tours and mountain expeditions. Their goal was to reach Otorten, a mountain in the northern Urals.

The journey started uneventfully as the group traveled by train, truck, and finally on foot, skiing towards their destination. On January 31, they arrived at a highland area and prepared to climb. Due to worsening weather conditions, which included snowstorms and decreased visibility, they deviated from their intended route. On

February 1, they set up a camp on the slopes of Kholat Syakhl, a name which, in the local Mansi language, means "Dead Mountain".

This was the last time the hikers were seen alive. When they failed to return as scheduled, friends and relatives grew increasingly concerned, and by February 20, a rescue operation was launched. What the search party found at Dyatlov Pass has fueled speculation and mystery ever since.

The hikers' tent, found badly damaged and half-covered in snow, appeared to have been cut open from the inside. The group's belongings and shoes were left behind in the tent, indicating a sudden and frantic departure. Footprints led down to the edge of the nearby woods, but disappeared after 500 meters.

The first two bodies, barefoot and dressed only in underwear, were found under a large pine tree near the remains of a fire. Broken branches up to 5 meters high suggested one of them had climbed up. Three more bodies, including Dyatlov's, were found between the tree and the camp, positioned as if they were trying to return to the tent.

Autopsies failed to provide clear answers. The cause of death was hypothermia, but the condition of the bodies, some with severe internal injuries, fractured skulls, and broken ribs, raised more questions than answers. Strangely, one of the victims had her tongue and eyes missing.

Several theories have been proposed over the years to explain the Dyatlov Pass Incident. These range from natural phenomena, such as an avalanche or infrasound caused by a rare type of wind, to more sensationalist theories involving military experiments, secret rocket testing, and even extraterrestrial encounters. The lack of conclusive evidence has only deepened the mystery.

In 2019, Russian authorities reopened the investigation into the incident, focusing on the three most likely scenarios: an avalanche, a slab avalanche, or a hurricane. However, the conclusion drawn was not definitive, and the mystery of the Dyatlov Pass Incident remains unsolved.

Graham Hodson

The Tunguska Event: A Blast from the Unknown

In the remote wilderness of Siberia, a mystery unfolded that has perplexed scientists and intrigued mystery lovers for over a century. This is the story of the Tunguska Event, a colossal explosion that occurred in 1908, which unleashed a force so powerful that it flattened trees and stunned wildlife over an area of 2,150 square kilometers. The enigma? Despite its massive impact, no definitive evidence of a meteoroid, comet, or any other usual suspect was ever found at the site.

On the morning of June 30, 1908, the tranquility of the sparsely populated Tunguska region was shattered by an explosion of apocalyptic proportions. Eyewitnesses hundreds of kilometers away reported seeing a bright bluish light, almost as bright as the sun, moving across the sky. This was followed by a flash and a sound similar to artillery fire. The shockwave knocked people off their feet and broke windows hundreds of kilometers away.

The explosion was so immense that it registered on seismic stations across Eurasia, and even caused fluctuations in atmospheric pressure as far away as Great Britain. What's more, in the nights that followed, strange phenomena were observed in the European and Asian skies: glowing clouds, colorful sunsets, and a strange luminescence in the night, which allowed people in some parts of Europe and Asia to read newspapers outdoors as late as midnight.

An expedition led by Russian mineralogist Leonid Kulik in the 1920s to the Tunguska region found a scene of devastation. Trees were flattened in a radial pattern, fanning out from the explosion's epicenter like spokes on a wheel. However, the most baffling aspect was the absence of an obvious impact crater. This absence fueled speculation and alternative theories about what caused the Tunguska Event.

The prevailing theory is that the explosion was caused by an airburst of a meteoroid or a comet about 5 to 10 kilometers above the Earth's surface. The object likely disintegrated in the atmosphere, explaining the lack of an impact crater. However, this explanation has not stopped alternative theories from flourishing, ranging from a black hole passing through Earth to an explosion of natural gas from within the Earth, and even to fanciful notions of alien intervention.

The Tunguska Event remains one of the 20th century's greatest natural mysteries. It represents not only a dramatic moment in Earth's history but also a poignant reminder of our planet's vulnerability to cosmic events. The explosion stands as a testament to the awesome and unpredictable powers that lie beyond our world and the mysteries that can unfold from the depths of the cosmos.

The Disappearance of Flight MH370: A Modern Aviation Enigma

On March 8, 2014, Malaysia Airlines Flight MH370, a Boeing 777 aircraft, took off from Kuala Lumpur International Airport, destined for Beijing with 239 people on board. Little did anyone know that this routine flight would turn into one of the most perplexing mysteries in modern aviation history. The disappearance of Flight MH370, and the subsequent international search and investigation efforts, would capture the world's attention and raise more questions than answers.

Flight MH370's journey began uneventfully. The aircraft, under the command of Captain Zaharie Ahmad Shah and First Officer Fariq Abdul Hamid, communicated normally with air traffic control as it climbed to its assigned cruising altitude. However, less than an hour into the flight, at 1:19 AM local time, the last voice communication from the cockpit was received. Shortly afterward, the aircraft vanished from radar screens over the South China Sea.

What makes the disappearance of MH370 particularly baffling is the series of events that followed its last contact. The aircraft's transponder, which communicates with ground radar, was switched off. Military radar continued to track the plane for a short while, as it turned sharply westward, deviating significantly from its planned flight path. This turn led the plane back over the Malay Peninsula, then out over the Andaman Sea.

In the days and weeks that followed, an unprecedented international search operation was launched. The search area spanned vast expanses of ocean, initially focusing on the South China Sea, then shifting to the Indian Ocean, west of Australia. This shift was based on analysis of automated satellite communications – or "pings" – between the aircraft and a satellite. This analysis suggested that MH370 continued flying for several hours after losing contact, following a southern trajectory into one of the most remote areas of the planet.

Various theories were proposed to explain MH370's fate. These ranged from mechanical failure and a deliberate act by the pilots or someone else on board, to a hijacking or a catastrophic event such as a fire. However, without physical evidence, these theories remained speculative.

In July 2015, the first piece of tangible evidence emerged. A wing part known as a flaperon, confirmed to be from Flight MH370, washed ashore on Réunion Island, far from the primary search area. Over the next few years, more debris was found along the coasts of the Indian Ocean, providing tragic and tangible proof that the aircraft had indeed ended in the ocean.

Despite the most extensive and expensive search in aviation history, the main wreckage of MH370 and its flight recorders have not been found, and the reasons for its disappearance remain unknown. The search officially ceased in January 2017, then resumed briefly in 2018 under private contract, but to no avail.

The disappearance of Flight MH370 is more than just an aviation mystery; it's a human tragedy. The lack of closure and answers has been agonizing for the families of the 239 passengers and crew. It has also challenged the aviation industry, leading to changes in flight tracking and communication technologies. As of now, the story of MH370 is an open chapter, a mystery that continues to intrigue and sadden the world.

Graham Hodson

Leonardo da Vinci, the Knights Templar, and the Priory of Sion: A Tale of Art, Mystery, and Legend

In a world rich with history and shrouded in mystery, there lived a man of unparalleled genius - Leonardo da Vinci. His story intertwines with two of the most enigmatic and intriguing groups in history: the Knights Templar and the Priory of Sion. Let us embark on a journey through time, exploring the fascinating connections and legends that bind these historical enigmas.

Leonardo da Vinci, born in 1452 in Vinci, Italy, was a polymath whose talents knew no bounds. He was a painter, sculptor, architect, scientist, and inventor. His artworks, like the Mona Lisa and The Last Supper, remain some of the most revered and studied masterpieces in the world. But Leonardo was more than just an artist; he was a visionary, a man whose curiosity and intellect delved into the mysteries of the universe.

Now, let's journey back a few centuries before Leonardo's time, to the era of the Crusades, where we encounter the Knights Templar. Founded in 1119, the Templars were a religious military order charged with protecting Christian pilgrims traveling to the Holy Land. They grew in power and wealth, becoming one of the most formidable organizations of the Middle Ages. However, their fortune took a dark turn, and in 1307, King Philip IV of France, in a move driven by greed and fear, disbanded the order and persecuted its members. The Templars, once protectors of Christendom, became subjects of legends and conspiracies, their fate shrouded in mystery.

Enter the Priory of Sion, a name that emerges in the 20th century, cloaked in mystery and intrigue. This supposed secret society claimed to have originated in the 11th century, with connections to the Knights Templar and a mission to protect sacred bloodlines and holy secrets. The Priory of Sion leapt into the public eye largely due to a series of documents, later revealed to be modern forgeries, and through the controversial book "Holy Blood, Holy Grail," which speculated on a hidden history involving Jesus Christ, Mary Magdalene, and their supposed bloodline.

The intertwining of Leonardo da Vinci with the Knights Templar and the Priory of Sion is a modern creation, a tapestry woven from threads of history, myth, and speculation. Some believe that Leonardo, with his vast knowledge and secretive nature, was a member of the Priory of Sion and that he embedded clues about these secrets in his art. These theories suggest that works like "The Last Supper" hold hidden symbols and codes revealing the true nature of the Holy Grail and the secrets guarded by the Priory.

While captivating, the connection between Leonardo, the Templars, and the Priory of Sion is more fiction than fact, born from a blend of historical intrigue and imaginative storytelling. The real Leonardo da Vinci was a man ahead of his time, whose works continue to inspire awe and wonder. The Knights Templar remain a symbol of the Crusades, their story a blend of historical fact and legend. And the Priory of Sion, largely a creation of modern myth-making, adds an element of mystery to this intriguing puzzle.

The Nazca Lines: Peru's Enigmatic Geoglyphs

Lying within the arid coastal plains of southern Peru, a mystery sprawls across the landscape, etched into the earth itself. These are the Nazca Lines, a series of large geoglyphs—designs or motifs produced on the ground—created by the ancient Nazca culture. Visible from the air, these lines form an array of intricate designs, including animals, plants, and geometric shapes, their purpose, creators, and methods of construction still subjects of fascination and debate.

The story of the Nazca Lines is a journey back in time, to a period between 500 BCE and 500 CE, when the Nazca people thrived in this region. The lines were made by removing the reddish-brown iron oxide-coated pebbles that cover the surface of the Nazca desert and revealing the light-colored earth underneath. These lines stretch across an area of about 1,000 square kilometers and include over 800 straight lines, 300 geometric figures, and 70 animal and plant designs, known as biomorphs.

Among these incredible figures, some of the most striking are the representations of animals and other entities: a spider, a hummingbird, a monkey, a whale, a lizard, and a human figure, often referred to as the Astronaut. Each figure varies in complexity and size, with the largest ones stretching over 200 meters in length.

The methods used to create these lines have baffled scientists and archaeologists for decades. The precision of the lines, some of which run straight over distances of up to 30 kilometers, is astounding, especially considering they were created without the ability to view them from the air. It's believed that the Nazca people may have used simple tools and surveying techniques to achieve the straight lines, possibly using wooden stakes to guide the design.

But why did the Nazca create these lines? This question has led to numerous theories. Some researchers suggest they were created as part of religious ceremonies or rituals, possibly linked to the heavens and water sources in this arid land. Others theorize they may have served astronomical purposes, functioning as a sort of observatory, aligning with the positions of stars and celestial bodies. There are also suggestions that they may have been part of a complex system for water, fertility, or agricultural rituals.

Despite various studies and theories, the true purpose of the Nazca Lines remains a mystery. This enigma is compounded by the fact that the Nazca culture left no written records, leaving us to piece together their story from the lines themselves and archaeological finds in the area.

Today, the Nazca Lines are a UNESCO World Heritage site, protected and studied, continuing to draw the curiosity of people from around the world. They are best viewed from the air, where their full splendor can be appreciated, a testament to the ingenuity and creativity of the Nazca people.

The Nazca Lines are a window into an ancient world, inviting us to ponder the capabilities and intentions of a civilization long gone. As we gaze upon these geoglyphs, whether in person or through images, we are connected to the past and to the mysteries that our ancestors left behind.

Graham Hodson

The Fate of the Roanoke Colony: A Historic Enigma

The fate of the Roanoke Colony stands as a haunting and enduring enigma. It's a tale of ambition, mystery, and sudden disappearance, set against the backdrop of the wild and uncharted lands of late 16th-century North America. The entire colony vanished, leaving behind only a cryptic message: "CROATOAN."

The story begins in 1587 when a group of about 115 English settlers, led by John White, arrived on Roanoke Island, off the coast of present-day North Carolina. Sponsored by Sir Walter Raleigh, this was not the first attempt to colonize the area, but it was to become the most infamous. The settlers, hoping to establish England's first permanent settlement in the New World, found themselves in a harsh and challenging environment.

Shortly after their arrival, tensions with the local Native American tribes grew. John White, the colony's leader and governor, was forced to return to England for supplies and reinforcements. However, his return was delayed by the outbreak of war with Spain, and it wasn't until 1590 that White could make the journey back to Roanoke.

What he found, or rather didn't find, has perplexed historians and archaeologists ever since. The colony was deserted; the settlers had vanished. The only clue was the word "CROATOAN" carved into a post of the fort and "CRO" etched into a nearby tree. All the houses and fortifications had been dismantled, suggesting the departure was not hasty or under duress.

The word "CROATOAN" was a reference to the Croatoan Island (now known as Hatteras Island), where a friendly Native American tribe lived. White took this as a sign that the colonists had moved there. However, a series of misfortunes, including bad weather and loss of ships, prevented White from ever reaching Croatoan Island to confirm this.

Over the centuries, the fate of the Roanoke settlers has been the subject of much speculation and investigation. Theories about what happened to them range from assimilation with local Native tribes to being lost at sea or falling victim to disease, starvation, or attacks by Spanish forces or hostile tribes.

Recent archaeological discoveries have provided some clues, suggesting that some of the settlers might have moved further inland or assimilated with local tribes, but no conclusive evidence has been found to fully explain what happened. The absence of any signs of a struggle or of a mass grave only adds to the mystery.

The Shroud of Turin: A Cloth Enshrouded in Mystery

Within the quiet city of Turin, Italy, lies one of the most debated and enigmatic relics in human history - the Shroud of Turin. Revered by some as the burial shroud of Jesus of Nazareth, the shroud is a long piece of linen cloth bearing the faint image of a man with wounds similar to those suffered during crucifixion. This relic has fascinated scholars, scientists, theologians, and the public alike for centuries, with its origins and authenticity sparking intense debate and investigation.

The story of the Shroud of Turin is a tapestry of history, faith, and science. The shroud first made its historical appearance in the mid-14th century in France. It was owned by a French knight, Geoffrey de Charny, who housed it in the church of Saint-Mary of Lirey. The shroud quickly became a matter of controversy, with some in the church believing it to be the genuine burial cloth of Jesus, while others declared it a clever forgery.

Over the centuries, the shroud changed hands multiple times, survived fires, and was moved to various locations, eventually finding its way to the Cathedral of Saint John the Baptist in Turin in 1578, where it has remained to this day. Despite its tumultuous history, the shroud has been a constant object of veneration, especially among the faithful, who see it as a tangible connection to the crucifixion and resurrection of Jesus.

The intrigue of the Shroud of Turin lies not only in its history but also in the mysterious image it bears. The faint imprint on the linen cloth shows the front and back of a bearded man, with markings that correspond to wounds traditionally associated with crucifixion: puncture wounds on the wrists and feet, lacerations, as if from scourging, and a wound on the side. This haunting image has been a subject of intense study and speculation. How was it formed? Is it a medieval artist's work, or could it be the authentic burial shroud of Jesus?

In 1988, the shroud was subjected to carbon-14 dating, a scientific method used to determine the age of artifacts. The tests, conducted by labs in Oxford, Zurich, and Arizona, concluded that the linen cloth was made between 1260 and 1390, suggesting it was a medieval forgery. However, these results have been contested by some who argue that the samples tested were contaminated or not representative of the whole cloth.

Moreover, the shroud's image itself remains a puzzle. Despite advances in technology, scientists have been unable to fully explain how the image was created. It does not appear to be painted or drawn; instead, it seems to be a result of some chemical reaction, perhaps related to a body's decomposition.

For believers, the Shroud of Turin is a symbol of faith, a physical manifestation of the biblical narratives. For skeptics, it is a fascinating medieval artifact, a testament to the artistic and scientific capabilities of that era. And for the undecided, it remains one of the most intriguing mysteries in the annals of religion and history.

The debate over the Shroud of Turin's authenticity continues, with new studies and research regularly conducted. Whether it is the genuine burial shroud of Jesus or an elaborate medieval forgery, the Shroud of Turin captures the imagination and curiosity of people across the world.

Graham Hodson

The Zodiac Killer

In the late 1960s and early 1970s, Northern California became the stage for a chilling drama of murder and mystery that continues to haunt the annals of American crime. The protagonist was an elusive, unidentified serial killer who called himself the Zodiac. The Zodiac Killer's reign of terror was marked not only by his brutal murders but also by the cryptic messages he sent to police and newspapers, taunting the authorities with clues that were as bewildering as they were chilling.

The Zodiac's grim saga began on the night of December 20, 1968, with the murder of two high school students, Betty Lou Jensen and David Faraday, on a lovers' lane in Vallejo, California. This brutal double homicide was only the beginning. Over the next several months, the killer struck repeatedly, targeting young couples and a lone cab driver, leaving a trail of death and fear in his wake.

What set the Zodiac Killer apart in the annals of crime was his disturbing correspondence with the media and police. He sent letters, often beginning with the chilling salutation "This is the Zodiac speaking," in which he claimed responsibility for the murders. These letters were frequently accompanied by cryptic ciphers, puzzles that he claimed held the key to his identity. The Zodiac boasted that his identity would be revealed if only the ciphers could be deciphered.

One of the Zodiac's ciphers, known as the Z340, remained unsolved for over 50 years, adding to the enigmatic nature of the case. The Zodiac's messages were a mix of taunts, threats, and bizarre ramblings, suggesting a killer who relished the attention and fear he generated. He claimed to be collecting his victims as "slaves for the afterlife" and seemed to revel in the public and police's inability to catch him.

The Zodiac's identity and motives have been the subject of intense speculation and numerous theories. Some have posited that he may have had military or law enforcement training, given his ability to evade capture. Others have suggested he was a disturbed individual, driven by a need for notoriety and a desire to instill fear. Despite the extensive investigation, which included several suspects and numerous forensic examinations, the Zodiac's true identity remains unknown.

The impact of the Zodiac Killer's crimes extends far beyond the horror of the murders themselves. He has become a part of the dark folklore of America, a symbol of the faceless, nameless terror that can strike from the shadows. His ability to elude capture and his boldness in taunting the police have made him the subject of countless articles, books, and movies, a figure of enduring fascination and horror.

The Wow! Signal: A Cosmic Whisper from the Unknown

On August 15, 1977, a 72-second burst of sound from the depths of space jolted the scientific community, marking the beginning of one of the most intriguing mysteries in the search for extraterrestrial intelligence. This event, known as the "Wow! Signal," is a perplexing piece of evidence in the cosmic puzzle, a brief brush with something unexplainable that has both tantalized and baffled astronomers for decades.

The story unfolds at the Ohio State University's Big Ear radio telescope, a massive structure dedicated to scanning the heavens for signs of extraterrestrial radio transmissions as part of the Search for Extraterrestrial Intelligence (SETI). That summer night, the telescope, under the watchful eye of astronomer Jerry R. Ehman, was conducting a routine scan of the sky. What it captured was anything but ordinary.

The signal, a strong, narrowband radio wave, appeared out of nowhere, bearing the hallmarks of potential extraterrestrial origin. It was unlike anything ever detected: intense, focused, and appearing to come from a fixed point in the sky in the constellation Sagittarius. Ehman, astounded by the data printout, circled the alphanumeric sequence representing the signal's intensity—6EQUJ5—and wrote "Wow!" in the margins, a simple exclamation that would become synonymous with one of the greatest enigmas in the world of astronomy.

The Wow! Signal was a singular event, lasting just over a minute and never repeating. It was detected on the 1420 MHz radio frequency, a band reserved for astronomical purposes and naturally emitted by hydrogen, the most abundant element in the universe. This frequency is part of the "water hole" spectrum, hypothesized as an ideal band for interstellar communication due to its clear transmission properties.

The uniqueness and characteristics of the signal prompted a wave of excitement and speculation. Was it a message from an advanced alien civilization? A cosmic beacon calling out across the void? Or was it something more mundane, like a reflection of a terrestrial signal or a natural but unknown astrophysical phenomenon?

Despite numerous attempts, the Wow! Signal has never been detected again. The Big Ear telescope continued to scan the same region of space for months afterward, but the mysterious signal remained a lone whisper in the cosmic night. Other telescopes, both before and after the incident, have scoured that part of the sky, yet the signal remains a singular event, a fleeting anomaly in the vast tapestry of the universe.

Many theories have been proposed to explain the Wow! Signal. Some suggest it could have been a transmission from an extraterrestrial probe or spacecraft, while others posit more natural explanations like a passing comet or a hydrogen cloud. However, none of these theories have been conclusively proven, and the signal's source remains a matter of speculation.

The Wow! Signal stands as a tantalizing hint of the potential for discovering extraterrestrial life, a beacon that momentarily bridged the immense gap between the stars. Whether it was a fleeting glitch, a secret message from a distant civilization, or something else entirely, the Wow! Signal remains one of the most compelling mysteries in the search for extraterrestrial intelligence, a cosmic question mark echoing through the ages.

Graham Hodson

Stonehenge: A Prehistoric Enigma in Stone

In the lush, rolling plains of Wiltshire, England, stands one of the world's most enigmatic and ancient structures - Stonehenge. This prehistoric monument, composed of a circle of towering stones set within earthworks, has captivated the human imagination for centuries. Its origins, purpose, and method of construction are shrouded in mystery, making Stonehenge a focal point for archaeological study, myth-making, and speculation.

Stonehenge's story begins in the Neolithic period, around 5,000 years ago. The construction of this monumental structure was not a single event but a series of episodes spanning over 1,500 years. The earliest phase of the monument, dating back to around 3000 BCE, started with the creation of a circular ditch and bank, with Aubrey holes, small round pits that may have held wooden posts or stones.

The most visually striking aspect of Stonehenge, the iconic standing stones, were erected in the center of the monument around 2500 BCE. These massive sarsen stones, some weighing as much as 25 tons, were arranged in an outer circle with a continuous run of lintels. Inside this circle stand five trilithons – pairs of tall, upright stones capped with a third horizontal stone – arranged in a horseshoe shape. Within this arrangement, there are smaller bluestones, brought from the Preseli Hills in Wales, over 150 miles away.

The transportation of these stones is one of the greatest mysteries of Stonehenge. How were Neolithic people, with their primitive tools and without the use of the wheel, able to move and erect these massive stones? Some theories suggest that the sarsens were transported over land, while the bluestones may have been moved by waterways and rollers. The precise alignment of the stones, particularly the horseshoe and heel stone, with the movements of the sun, suggests a deep understanding of astronomical phenomena.

Over the centuries, Stonehenge has been a site of continuous speculation and sacred associations. Early historians, like Geoffrey of Monmouth in the 12th century, attributed Stonehenge to the wizard Merlin, claiming it was magically transported from Ireland. In the modern era, interpretations have ranged from astronomical observatory to religious temple, from a place of healing to a site of ancestral worship or burial.

Recent archaeological investigations have shed light on the people who built Stonehenge. Analysis of burial mounds nearby suggests that it was an area inhabited by an elite ruling class, possibly a site of pilgrimage. Archaeological evidence shows that people came from as far as Scotland to visit Stonehenge, indicating its importance in the Neolithic landscape.

Today, Stonehenge continues to be a place of wonder and mystery. It attracts thousands of visitors every year, including those who gather for the summer and winter solstices, when the sun aligns perfectly with the stones. For many, Stonehenge is a spiritual place, a link to our distant ancestors and their enigmatic ways.

The Lost Colony of Paititi: In Search of a Hidden Inca City

Deep in the dense, uncharted jungles of Peru, a legend persists about a lost city of immense wealth and splendor, a hidden refuge of the Inca civilization - the city of Paititi. For centuries, explorers, treasure hunters, and historians have been captivated by the tale of this mythical city, said to hold untold riches and secrets of a bygone era. The story of Paititi is a tantalizing blend of history, myth, and adventure, a quest for discovery that continues to allure and mystify.

The legend of Paititi emerged in the wake of the Spanish Conquest of the Inca Empire in the 16th century. As the conquistadors plundered the Inca's gold and silver, stories began to circulate about a city far in the jungle, where the Incas had hidden their treasures from the invaders. Paititi, as it came to be known, was described as a place of immense wealth, filled with gold, precious stones, and artifacts of incredible artistic and cultural value.

The first recorded mention of Paititi dates back to the early 1600s in the writings of a Spanish missionary named Father Andres Lopez. In his accounts, Lopez describes a large city rich in gold, silver, and jewels, located in the jungle east of the Andes Mountains. According to legend, this city was the last refuge of the Inca nobility who fled Cusco to escape Spanish conquest.

Over the years, the legend of Paititi grew, fueling numerous expeditions into the Peruvian Amazon. Explorers and adventurers from all over the world ventured into the dense rainforest, braving harsh conditions, and hostile terrain, driven by the promise of discovering a city lost in time. Despite these efforts, no one has been able to provide definitive proof of Paititi's existence.

The search for Paititi has not been without its challenges and controversies. The dense jungle, remote location, and lack of concrete historical evidence make the search extraordinarily difficult. Satellite imagery and modern technology have offered new ways to explore the region from above, leading to the discovery of previously unknown archaeological sites, but Paititi remains elusive.

Some archaeologists believe that Paititi may not be a single city but rather a larger region encompassing a network of smaller settlements and ceremonial centers. This theory suggests that Paititi might represent a cultural and religious hub rather than a city of gold as popularly imagined.

Despite the skepticism of many experts, the legend of Paititi continues to captivate the imagination. It's a story that speaks to the allure of the unknown and the human spirit of exploration. The quest for Paititi is not just about finding a lost city of gold; it's about uncovering a piece of human history, a glimpse into an ancient civilization that still holds many secrets.

Graham Hodson

The Rongorongo Writing of Easter Island: An Undeciphered Enigma

On the remote and windswept Easter Island, known to its indigenous people as Rapa Nui, lies one of the most intriguing linguistic mysteries of our time: the Rongorongo script. Discovered in the 19th century, Rongorongo is a system of glyphs, a script that is unique to the island. It consists of intricate, carved symbols on wooden tablets, a code from the past that has resisted all attempts at deciphering. The story of Rongorongo is not just about a set of inscriptions; it's a journey into a lost culture and a script that might hold the secrets of a fascinating civilization.

Easter Island, famous for its colossal stone statues called moai, was first visited by Europeans in 1722. The Dutch explorer Jacob Roggeveen encountered a thriving culture with a complex social structure and rich traditions. However, by the time the Rongorongo inscriptions were discovered in the 19th century, the island's society had undergone dramatic changes due to disease, slave raids, and colonial impact, leading to the loss of many aspects of the traditional Rapa Nui culture.

The first recorded mention of the Rongorongo script was in 1864 by Eugene Eyraud, a French missionary. He described seeing tablets with hieroglyphic writing, which the islanders seemed to read with great reverence. Unfortunately, by this time, the knowledge of reading the Rongorongo glyphs had been largely lost among the Rapa Nui people.

The tablets feature a system of glyphs, with each character distinct and complex, ranging from geometric shapes to representations of human figures, animals, and plants. The script is unique among ancient writing systems for being written in a reverse boustrophedon manner; the reader must turn the tablet 180 degrees at the end of each line to continue reading.

The purpose and content of the Rongorongo writing remain a mystery. Some researchers believe that the inscriptions could be a form of proto-writing or ideographic symbols, representing a type of proto-writing system rather than a true language. Others suggest that the tablets hold genealogies, legends, or ritual chants. The Rapa Nui oral tradition speaks of 'talking boards' and 'singing wood', suggesting that the tablets were used in chants and were part of religious ceremonies.

The challenge of deciphering Rongorongo is compounded by the small number of tablets that have survived and the loss of cultural context. Many tablets were lost or destroyed in the 19th century, with only about two dozen known to exist today in museums and private collections around the world. The lack of a bilingual text, like the Rosetta Stone which was crucial for deciphering Egyptian hieroglyphs, makes the task even more daunting.

The Rongorongo script of Easter Island continues to be a subject of fascination and debate among linguists, archaeologists, and historians. Its undeciphered glyphs hold the potential to unlock a wealth of knowledge about the Rapa Nui civilization and its mysterious past. Whether it's a true writing system that records the history and beliefs of the Easter Island people, or a more symbolic form of expression, Rongorongo remains one of the few undeciphered scripts in the world, a tantalizing enigma that continues to challenge and intrigue.

The Oak Island Enigma: In Search of Buried Secrets

Nestled on the foggy shores of Nova Scotia, Canada, lies a small, wooded island wrapped in centuries of mystery and intrigue. This is Oak Island, the center of the world's longest and most expensive treasure hunt. The legend of Oak Island is a captivating mix of history, mystery, and the allure of untold riches. It's a tale that has seen fortunes spent, lives lost, and yet, the island continues to guard its secret with inscrutable silence.

The story of Oak Island's treasure begins in 1795 when a young man named Daniel McGinnis discovered an unusual depression in the ground while exploring the island. Intrigued, McGinnis, along with friends John Smith and Anthony Vaughan, began to dig. As they excavated, they found a layer of flagstones, a series of wooden platforms at regular intervals, and even what seemed to be the remains of a pickaxe. The deeper they dug, the more elaborate the construction appeared. However, after reaching about 30 feet, they were forced to abandon their dig.

The mystery deepened in the following decades as various individuals and companies attempted to uncover what lay at the bottom of what became known as the "Money Pit." Each attempt seemed to bring more intrigue and complexity. Reports of booby traps, flooding tunnels, and cryptic symbols fueled speculation that the island hid an extraordinary treasure. Ideas of what the treasure could be range from pirate loot, such as that of Captain Kidd or Blackbeard, to religious artifacts like the Holy Grail or the Ark of the Covenant, and even manuscripts that could rewrite history.

Despite the numerous expeditions and the advanced technology deployed, the Oak Island treasure has remained elusive. The island has yielded some tantalizing clues: links of gold chain, old coins, parchment paper, and a stone slab inscribed with mysterious symbols. Yet, the core of the mystery, the main treasure, remains untouched.

The Oak Island mystery is not just about treasure. It's also a story of human ambition, persistence, and the unquenchable thirst for the unknown. The island has seen its share of tragedy and triumph. The pursuit of its secrets has claimed lives and fortunes, sparking a legend that has only grown with each passing year. For some, the island is a puzzle to be solved, a challenge to human ingenuity and perseverance. For others, it's a tantalizing hint that our world still hides secrets and wonders beyond our understanding.

As the sun sets over the mysterious waters surrounding Oak Island, the legend continues to attract treasure hunters, historians, and mystery enthusiasts. The island, with its centuries-old riddles, stands as a testament to the enduring allure of the unknown, a siren call to those who seek to uncover the secrets buried beneath its soil.

Graham Hodson

Hollywood's Dark Rose: The Black Dahlia Murder

The story of the Black Dahlia murder unfolds in post-World War II Los Angeles, a city of glitz and glamour, but also of dark alleys and broken dreams. It was here, in this city of stark contrasts, that the gruesome murder of Elizabeth Short, dubbed the Black Dahlia, became one of Hollywood's most notorious and enduring unsolved mysteries.

Elizabeth Short, a young woman with aspirations of stardom, arrived in Los Angeles with the same glittering hopes that drew many to Hollywood. Her striking appearance and jet-black hair, often styled in a flower-like coiffure, earned her the nickname "The Black Dahlia" in the sensationalist press. However, behind the aspiring actress's enigmatic smile lay a tale that would end in tragedy.

On the morning of January 15, 1947, Short's lifeless body was found in a vacant lot in the Leimert Park neighborhood of Los Angeles, her remains severed at the waist and horrifyingly mutilated. The body was posed in a grotesque display, drained of blood, with cuts from the corners of her mouth to her ears, creating a haunting, Joker-like grin. This chilling tableau sparked a media frenzy, with newspapers battling to outdo each other with lurid details and sensational headlines.

The ensuing investigation by the Los Angeles Police Department was extensive, involving hundreds of officers and numerous suspects. The case quickly became mired in a web of rumors, false leads, and dead ends. Everyone from local gangsters to a plethora of boyfriends, and even prominent figures, found themselves entangled in the investigation. Despite the numerous suspects and theories, no one was ever charged, and the murder remained unsolved.

The Black Dahlia murder was more than a mere homicide; it was a symbol of the dark underbelly of Hollywood, a place where fame and fortune could just as easily lead to ruin and despair. Elizabeth Short's murder became a cautionary tale, a story that peeled back the glamorous façade of Hollywood to reveal a world of noirish intrigue and danger.

Over the years, the case has become the subject of countless books, films, and documentaries, each attempting to shed light on this dark mystery. The Black Dahlia murder remains a topic of fascination, not only for its brutality but for what it represents: the intersection of innocence and corruption, of dreams and nightmares. Elizabeth Short's unsolved murder continues to haunt the collective memory, a ghostly presence in Hollywood's history, an enigma that remains as captivating as it is chilling.

The Loch Ness Monster: Scotland's Enduring Legend

In the misty waters of Loch Ness, a deep, expansive lake in the Scottish Highlands, lurks a mystery as enduring as it is elusive. This is the domain of the Loch Ness Monster, or "Nessie," a creature of legend and folklore that has captured the imagination of believers and skeptics alike. The tale of Nessie is not just a story of a possible creature lurking in the depths; it's a narrative that intertwines history, science, and the timeless allure of the unknown.

The legend of the Loch Ness Monster is an ancient one, stretching back over a thousand years. Early accounts of a creature in Loch Ness date back to the 6th century, in a story about St. Columba, an Irish monk who supposedly encountered a monstrous beast in the river Ness. However, it wasn't until the 20th century that Nessie captured the public's imagination.

The modern legend began to take shape in 1933, with a sighting by a local couple who reported seeing an enormous animal rolling and plunging in the lake. The story was picked up by the media, and soon, Loch Ness was swarming with tourists and monster hunters. In 1934, the mystery deepened with the publication of the iconic "Surgeon's Photograph," which appeared to show a serpentine head and neck emerging from the water. This image cemented the creature's place in popular culture, although it was later revealed to be a hoax.

Since then, there have been countless sightings, photos, and sonar readings, each adding to the legend. Descriptions of Nessie vary, with some depicting it as a plesiosaur-like creature with a long neck, others as a large eel or fish. Theories about its true nature range from surviving dinosaurs to large fish, giant eels, or even optical illusions caused by floating logs or gas bubbles.

Scientific interest in Nessie has led to numerous expeditions and studies. In recent years, scientists have used DNA sampling of the lake's waters to catalog its biodiversity, hoping to find evidence of an unknown species. While these studies have provided valuable insight into the ecology of Loch Ness, the mystery of Nessie remains unsolved.

The Loch Ness Monster is more than a potential undiscovered creature; it is a symbol of the human fascination with the mysterious and the unexplained. Nessie represents the possibility of undiscovered wonders in our world, a reminder that there may still be mysteries lurking in the unexplored corners of our planet. The legend of the Loch Ness Monster endures, a captivating blend of myth, mystery, and the allure of the uncharted, forever inviting us to wonder what might be hiding beneath the dark waters of Loch Ness.

59

Graham Hodson

The Lost City of Atlantis: A Tale Submerged in Mystery

Among the most captivating and enduring mysteries of human history is the legend of the Lost City of Atlantis. Described by the ancient Greek philosopher Plato more than 2,400 years ago, Atlantis has ignited the imagination of explorers, archaeologists, and dreamers, becoming a symbol of advanced, prehistoric civilizations lost to time and the sea. The story of Atlantis is a tapestry woven from history, philosophy, and myth, a narrative that has evolved and expanded over centuries, leaving us to ponder whether this fabled city ever existed.

Plato introduced the tale of Atlantis in two of his dialogues, "Timaeus" and "Critias," written around 360 BC. According to Plato, Atlantis was a large island located beyond the "Pillars of Hercules," what we now call the Strait of Gibraltar. He described it as a paradise of unparalleled beauty, rich in resources, and inhabited by a noble and powerful race.

The heart of Atlantis, as told by Plato, was a marvel of architecture and engineering. The city was composed of concentric islands separated by wide moats and linked by a canal that penetrated to the center. The dwellings and structures were made of a striking combination of red, black, and white stone, adorned with precious metals and exotic fauna. The Atlanteans, blessed with an abundance of natural resources, created a utopian society, with an advanced civilization, formidable naval power, and a peaceful, prosperous way of life.

However, Plato's Atlantis was not destined to endure. He narrated that over time, the Atlanteans became morally corrupt, their hearts filled with greed and lust for power. In response to their hubris, the gods sent one terrible night of fire and earthquakes that caused Atlantis to sink into the sea, disappearing forever.

The exact purpose of Plato's Atlantis story remains a topic of debate among scholars. Some interpret it as a parable or allegory, a cautionary tale about the dangers of moral and spiritual decay. Others believe Plato intended it as a historical account, a true story passed down through generations.

Over the centuries, the story of Atlantis has been embellished and reshaped, with various cultures adding their own interpretations and details. It has been connected to diverse geographical locations, from the Mediterranean Sea to the Caribbean, and even Antarctica. Each proposed site for Atlantis comes with its own set of hypotheses and evidence, but none have been definitively proven.

Modern advancements in archaeology and oceanography have allowed for extensive exploration of the ocean depths, yet no trace of Atlantis has been conclusively identified.

The Location of Cleopatra's Tomb: An Ancient Egyptian Enigma

Of all the people throughout ancient history, few figures are as captivating and enigmatic as Cleopatra, the last active ruler of the Ptolemaic Kingdom of Egypt. Famed for her intelligence, charisma, beauty, and political acumen, Cleopatra's life was marked by alliances and romances with powerful Roman figures such as Julius Caesar and Mark Antony. Yet, despite her enduring fame, the location of the tomb of Cleopatra VII remains one of history's great unsolved mysteries, a hidden secret of the ancient world that has eluded discovery for centuries.

Cleopatra's life, and her eventual tragic death in 30 BC, is a story steeped in drama and intrigue. Following the defeat at the Battle of Actium and the subsequent fall of Egypt to Roman rule, Cleopatra and her lover, Mark Antony, retreated to Alexandria. According to historical accounts, after Mark Antony took his own life following a false report of Cleopatra's death, Cleopatra herself succumbed to a self-inflicted venomous snake bite, choosing death over submission to the Roman victor, Octavian, later known as Augustus.

The mystery surrounding Cleopatra's final resting place began almost immediately after her death. Ancient sources, including the Roman historian Plutarch, suggest that Cleopatra and Mark Antony were buried together in a tomb befitting their status. However, the exact location of this tomb has been lost to history. Over the millennia, countless theories and expeditions have sought to uncover the famed queen's final resting place, but to no avail.

The search for Cleopatra's tomb has been complicated by several factors. The ancient city of Alexandria, where Cleopatra reigned and where many believe her tomb to be located, has changed significantly over the centuries. Earthquakes, tsunamis, and the rising sea level have altered the landscape, submerging parts of the ancient city underwater and making archaeological exploration challenging.

Various locations in and around Alexandria have been proposed as the site of Cleopatra's tomb. One prominent theory suggests that she was buried in a temple complex known as Taposiris Magna, west of Alexandria. This site has been the focus of extensive excavations, which have unearthed numerous artifacts and a series of tombs, but Cleopatra's tomb remains elusive.

Another theory posits that Cleopatra's tomb might be located beneath the modern city of Alexandria. Over the centuries, the city has been built over the top of the ancient remains, making archaeological investigations difficult. Some speculate that the tomb could be hidden beneath the bustling streets and buildings of contemporary Alexandria, waiting to be discovered.

The search for Cleopatra's tomb is not just an archaeological quest; it's a journey into the heart of ancient Egyptian history and culture. Cleopatra is a symbol of Egypt's last stand against the encroaching power of Rome, and her tomb, if found, would offer unprecedented insights into the final days of the Ptolemaic Dynasty and the end of an era in Egyptian history.

Graham Hodson

The Tale of the Smalls Lighthouse: A Haunting Beacon in the Sea

Off the rugged coast of Pembrokeshire, Wales, perched on a solitary rock in the midst of treacherous waters, stands the Smalls Lighthouse. This remote beacon has become known not just for guiding sailors through perilous seas, but also as the setting for one of the most haunting and disturbing tales in maritime history. The story, which unfolded in the early 19th century, is a chilling narrative of isolation, death, and madness, centered on two lighthouse keepers and a fateful storm.

In the early 1800s, the Smalls Lighthouse was manned by two keepers, as was customary at the time. The lighthouse's location, some 20 miles off the coast, made it one of the most isolated and dangerous postings for keepers. In such remote settings, the men were completely dependent on each other for survival and companionship, often under extremely challenging conditions.

The story begins with two such keepers: Thomas Howell and Thomas Griffith. They were tasked with the important job of maintaining the light, ensuring that it shone brightly to warn passing ships of the perilous rocks below. Life at the lighthouse was monotonous and challenging, with the men confined to the small space, braving the elements and the loneliness that came with their job.

Tragedy struck when one of the men, Thomas Griffith, died suddenly. This left Howell in an unimaginable situation. Alone, miles from shore, with no means of communication and stuck with the body of his deceased colleague. The rules of the time dictated that a dead body had to be kept until authorities could conduct an inquest, to rule out foul play. In his desperation and isolation, Howell decided to construct a makeshift coffin and lashed it to the outside of the lighthouse.

However, nature had other plans. A fierce storm hit, battering the lighthouse with wind and waves. The storm was so intense that it broke the coffin apart, exposing Griffith's corpse. In a macabre twist, the decomposing body's arm became dislodged in such a way that it appeared to be beckoning. Howell, trapped in the lighthouse with the storm raging outside and the ghastly sight of his former colleague, was driven to the brink of insanity.

Howell spent days in these horrifying conditions, his sanity hanging by a thread. When the weather finally calmed and a relief boat was able to reach the lighthouse, the rescue crew found a deeply traumatized Howell, whose relief at being rescued was overshadowed by the trauma of his experience.

The incident at the Smalls Lighthouse had a profound impact on lighthouse operations. It led to a change in policy, mandating that three keepers be posted instead of two, to ensure that such a situation would never occur again. This policy remained in place until the automation of lighthouses in the 20th century.

The tale of the Smalls Lighthouse is more than just a ghost story; it's a poignant reminder of the psychological strains faced by lighthouse keepers, the men who lived on the fringes of society, battling loneliness and the elements to keep sailors safe. The story of Howell and Griffith's harrowing experience continues to echo through time, a haunting narrative of isolation, mortality, and the human psyche pushed to its limits.

Dark Matter and Dark Energy: The Cosmic Shadows

In the vast expanse of the universe, there lie two of the most profound mysteries in the field of astrophysics: dark matter and dark energy. These enigmatic components of the cosmos, invisible and intangible, defy our understanding of physics and the universe. Together, dark matter and dark energy compose about 95% of the total mass-energy content of the universe, yet their nature remains one of the great unsolved puzzles in science.

Dark matter, a term first coined in the 1930s by Swiss astrophysicist Fritz Zwicky, refers to a type of matter that does not emit, absorb, or reflect light, making it invisible to current astronomical instruments. The existence of dark matter was proposed to explain the gravitational effects observed in galaxies and galaxy clusters that could not be accounted for by the amount of observable matter alone.

The evidence for dark matter comes from various astronomical observations. One of the key pieces of evidence is the rotation of galaxies. According to the laws of physics, the speed with which stars in a galaxy orbit its center should decrease with distance from the center. However, observations show that stars in the outer regions of galaxies orbit at the same speed as those near the center, suggesting the presence of an unseen mass - dark matter - exerting its gravitational influence.

Another compelling evidence comes from the phenomenon of gravitational lensing, where the gravity of a massive object, like a galaxy cluster, bends the light of more distant galaxies. This bending of light, observed by the Hubble Space Telescope and other instruments, can be used to map the distribution of dark matter, revealing massive structures that cannot be detected through conventional astronomical methods.

While dark matter remains elusive, dark energy is an even greater mystery. The concept of dark energy emerged from the discovery that the universe is not just expanding, but its expansion is accelerating. This startling revelation, based on observations of distant supernovae in the late 1990s, contradicted the then-prevailing notion that the expansion of the universe was slowing down due to gravitational pull.

Dark energy, which constitutes about 68% of the universe, is theorized to be a form of energy permeating all of space, pushing galaxies apart and driving the acceleration of the universe's expansion. Its properties and origins are unknown, and it challenges the very fundamentals of physics. Theoretical models, including the cosmological constant proposed by Albert Einstein and the concept of quintessence, a dynamic field, are some of the attempts to explain dark energy. However, a definitive understanding remains elusive.

The quest to understand dark matter and dark energy is not just a scientific endeavor; it's a journey into the unknown realms of the cosmos. These mysterious components challenge our understanding of the nature of the universe, gravity, and the fundamental laws of physics.

Advancements in technology and observational techniques are gradually shedding light on these cosmic shadows. Projects like the Large Hadron Collider, space telescopes, and dark matter detectors deep underground are at the forefront of this exploration.

Graham Hodson

The Taos Hum: A Mysterious Symphony of the Unknown

In the quaint town of Taos, nestled in the scenic landscape of New Mexico, there resonates a mystery as perplexing as it is unsettling. This mystery, known as the Taos Hum, involves a persistent and invasive low-frequency sound heard by some residents and visitors, a sound whose origin remains a baffling enigma. The phenomenon, first reported in the early 1990s, extends beyond the borders of Taos, with similar reports emerging from various parts of the world, turning it into a global mystery of unexplained acoustics.

The Taos Hum, as described by those who have heard it, is a low, distant, rumbling sound, likened to a diesel engine idling in the distance. It's a sound that penetrates through walls and windows, more felt than heard, a relentless hum that can be both maddening and elusive. What makes the hum particularly mystifying is its selective audibility - only a small percentage of the Taos population report hearing it. This selective perception has led to a wide range of theories, ranging from the scientific to the speculative.

The emergence of the Taos Hum prompted investigations by researchers and scientists, including a team from the University of New Mexico and the Los Alamos National Laboratory. They conducted a series of surveys and experiments to try to pinpoint the source of the sound but came up empty-handed. The lack of concrete findings fueled more speculation and interest, transforming the Taos Hum into a subject of national intrigue.

Theories about the Taos Hum are as varied as they are imaginative. Some researchers suggest that the hum could be a form of low-frequency sound, or infrasound, generated by geological or atmospheric phenomena. Others propose more unconventional sources, such as electromagnetic activity, secret military experiments, or even extraterrestrial technology. However, none of these theories have been conclusively proven, and the hum remains an acoustic mystery.

The Taos Hum is not an isolated phenomenon. Similar unexplained sounds have been reported in various locations worldwide, including in the United Kingdom, Australia, and Canada. These global occurrences, often referred to as 'The Hum', share common characteristics with the Taos Hum, including the low-frequency nature of the sound and the fact that only a small percentage of the population in these areas report hearing it.

The elusive nature of the hum has led to a variety of psychological and physiological explanations as well. Some scientists have explored the possibility that the hum could be a case of mass hysteria or a form of auditory hallucination. Others consider it might be a manifestation of tinnitus, an auditory condition characterized by the perception of sound when no external sound is present. However, these explanations don't account for the fact that the hum is often heard only in specific locations and conditions.

The Taos Hum remains one of the more puzzling and lesser-understood phenomena in the realm of unexplained mysteries. It is a reminder of the limitations of our understanding of the world around us and the complexities of sensory perception. For those who hear it, the hum is a source of intrigue, frustration, and fascination—a continuous whisper from the unknown, echoing across the serene landscapes of Taos and beyond.

D.B. Cooper: The Skyjacker Who Vanished Into Thin Air

This is the tale of D.B. Cooper. His story is one of audacity, cunning, and an almost cinematic escape, a narrative that weaves its way through the skies of the Pacific Northwest. D.B. Cooper's identity and fate remain one of the greatest unsolved mysteries in FBI history, a shadowy figure who achieved an impossible heist and vanished into thin air.

Our story begins on a cold afternoon on November 24, 1971, at Portland International Airport. A man carrying a black attaché case approached the counter of Northwest Orient Airlines and purchased a one-way ticket to Seattle. He gave his name as Dan Cooper, a nondescript name for a man who would soon become anything but. Aboard Flight 305, a Boeing 727, Cooper was a quiet, unassuming figure, dressed in a dark suit with a black tie and white shirt.

As the plane ascended, Cooper revealed his true intentions. He passed a note to a flight attendant, calmly informing her that he had a bomb in his briefcase and was hijacking the plane. Showing her the wires and red sticks inside his case, Cooper made his demands: $200,000 in cash, four parachutes, and a fuel truck standing by in Seattle to refuel the plane for a getaway.

Upon landing in Seattle, Cooper's demands were met. The passengers were released, and the plane, now refueled and with only Cooper, the pilot, co-pilot, a flight attendant, and a flight engineer on board, took off again. Cooper directed them to fly towards Mexico City at a low altitude and reduced speed.

Then, in the cover of the night and the roar of the aircraft's engines, Cooper did the unthinkable. He strapped on a parachute, tied the money bag to himself, lowered the plane's aft stairs, and leapt into the stormy night sky. The plane later landed safely, but Cooper had disappeared into the darkness, his fate a mystery.

The ensuing manhunt was extensive. The FBI launched one of the most exhaustive investigations in its history, code-named "Norjak." They analyzed everything from the ransom money to Cooper's tie, which he left on the plane, and interviewed hundreds of suspects. Despite their efforts, Cooper's true identity and fate remained elusive.

In 1980, a boy found a rotting package containing $5,800 with serial numbers matching the ransom money on the banks of the Columbia River. This discovery fueled further speculation but offered no conclusive answers.

The legend of D.B. Cooper has become a part of popular culture, inspiring books, films, and songs. He is seen by some as a folk hero, a man who committed the perfect crime and vanished, and by others as a reckless criminal who endangered lives. His case invites us to ponder the limits of human daring and the mysteries that one man can leave behind.

The D.B. Cooper hijacking remains a captivating unsolved mystery, a story of a ghostly hijacker who stepped out into the night and into the realm of legend. Whether he survived the jump or not, Cooper's story is a tale of intrigue and audacity, a narrative that continues to challenge and intrigue, a reminder of the enduring appeal of an unsolvable mystery.

Graham Hodson

The Isdal Woman: Norway's Deepening Mystery

In the files of unsolved mysteries, the case of the Isdal Woman stands out as one of the most intriguing and haunting. The story begins on a chilly November day in 1970 in the Isdalen Valley near Bergen, Norway. It's a tale that weaves together elements of mystery, espionage, and identity, leaving a trail of questions that remain unanswered to this day.

On November 29, 1970, a professor and his two daughters, out for a Sunday hike in the Isdalen ("Ice Valley"), stumbled upon a chilling scene. There, among the rocks and icy crags, lay the charred remains of a woman. The scene was peculiar and unsettling: the woman's hands were clenched up against her chest, and several objects were carefully arranged around her body – empty bottles, a packed lunch, an umbrella, and a watch.

The police investigation that followed only deepened the mystery. The labels on the woman's clothes were removed, and distinct marks suggested that her eyebrows had been pencilled in to alter her appearance. Even more baffling, all identifying marks and labels on the objects surrounding her were erased or rubbed off.

The autopsy revealed that the woman had died from a combination of carbon monoxide poisoning and sleeping pill overdose. There were traces of nearly 50 sleeping pills in her system, some not yet dissolved. Soot in her lungs suggested she was alive as she burned, and the cause of death was declared as suicide, though many details suggested otherwise.

The plot thickened as investigators dug deeper. The woman had left behind a trail of aliases and false identities. In the weeks before her death, she had traveled around Norway and other parts of Europe, checking into hotels under different names, all with false addresses. Hotel staff remembered her as well-dressed, with dark hair and a foreign accent. She was elusive, often changing rooms and requesting to be placed away from other guests.

What stood out most was her behavior. Witnesses described her as constantly looking over her shoulder, as if she were on the run or expecting someone. In her suitcases, discovered at a Bergen railway station, there were wigs, several pairs of glasses, and money from different countries – suggestive of someone with a secret life, perhaps espionage.

Over the years, numerous theories have emerged about the Isdal Woman's identity and the reason for her death. Was she a spy, caught in the Cold War intrigues between East and West? Was it a case of murder, or did she indeed take her own life, and if so, why?

The Norwegian police reopened the case in 2016, using modern technology to analyze the woman's remains and the items found with her. Despite these efforts, her identity remains a mystery. The DNA analysis has not matched any missing person reports, and the Isdal Woman's true identity and the circumstances of her death remain shrouded in mystery.

The Isdal Woman remains an enigmatic figure, her story a haunting blend of mystery, tragedy, and unanswered questions, echoing through the annals of unsolved cases.

UFO Sightings: The Enduring Enigma of the Skies

For decades, the skies above us have been a source of mystery and speculation, dotted not just with stars and satellites, but also, according to many, with unidentified flying objects, or UFOs. These sightings, reported by individuals from all walks of life, have sparked curiosity, skepticism, and intense debate. The story of UFO sightings is a fascinating tapestry of unexplained phenomena, government secrecy, and the endless quest to understand what lies beyond our world.

The modern era of UFO sightings began in the mid-20th century, although historical accounts suggest that humans have observed mysterious objects in the sky for centuries. The term "UFO" was popularized in the 1950s, originally used to describe any airborne object whose nature could not be immediately identified. Over time, it has become synonymous with extraterrestrial spacecraft, a concept that has firmly rooted itself in popular culture.

One of the earliest and most influential incidents in UFO history occurred in 1947 when a civilian pilot named Kenneth Arnold reported seeing nine high-speed objects near Mount Rainier in Washington State. Arnold described the objects as saucer-like, coining the term "flying saucers," which would become a staple in UFO lore. His account was widely reported and sparked a wave of sightings across the United States.

Perhaps the most famous UFO incident is the 1947 Roswell UFO incident, in which an object crashed near Roswell, New Mexico. Initially reported as a "flying disc," the U.S. military later stated it was a weather balloon. Over the years, this explanation was contested by many, leading to theories of a government cover-up and the recovery of extraterrestrial technology and occupants. Roswell has since become synonymous with UFO conspiracy theories and is a central element of UFO folklore.

UFO sightings have been reported worldwide, with many being documented and investigated by governments and independent organizations. Some of these sightings have been explained as natural phenomena, man-made objects, or optical illusions. However, a significant number of reports remain unexplained, fueling speculation about their origins and nature.

In recent years, the topic of UFOs has gained renewed attention and legitimacy. Leaked videos and accounts from military personnel have shown unidentified objects exhibiting speed and maneuverability beyond known human-made aircraft capabilities. These revelations have led to official acknowledgments from government agencies, acknowledging the existence of unidentified aerial phenomena (UAP) and the need for further investigation.

The story of UFO sightings is a journey through the unknown, where the line between science and science fiction blurs. Whether UFOs are misidentified earthly objects, secret military projects, or indeed visitors from other worlds, they remain one of the most captivating unsolved mysteries of our time.

Graham Hodson

The Easter Island Statues: Mysteries Carved in Stone

On the remote and windswept Easter Island, known as Rapa Nui to its indigenous people, stand one of the world's most enigmatic creations - the Moai statues. These colossal stone figures, carved centuries ago, have captured the world's imagination and puzzled archaeologists and historians for decades. The story of the Easter Island statues is not just a tale of an ancient and sophisticated civilization but also a narrative filled with mystery, particularly regarding how these massive statues were transported and erected across the island.

Easter Island, located in the southeastern Pacific Ocean, was first settled by Polynesian navigators around 1200 AD. The Moai statues, which number over 900, were carved from the island's volcanic tuff between the 13th and 16th centuries. These statues, with their oversized heads, somber expressions, and imposing stature, can reach up to 33 feet in height and weigh as much as 82 tons. The largest unfinished statue, known as "El Gigante," is about 69 feet tall and weighs around 270 tons.

The mystery surrounding the Moai lies not in their construction but in their transportation and erection. The statues were carved at Rano Raraku, a volcanic crater that served as a quarry. From there, they were moved to various ceremonial platforms called ahu, which are scattered around the island's perimeter. The question that baffles experts is: how were these giant statues, some weighing several tons, transported across the island without the use of modern machinery or wheels, which the Rapa Nui people did not have?

Several theories have been proposed to explain this feat. One of the earliest theories suggested that the statues were moved in a horizontal position on rollers or sledges made from tree trunks. However, this theory led to another question: did the transportation of the Moai lead to the deforestation of Easter Island? Some researchers have suggested that the overuse of trees for moving the statues contributed to ecological collapse on the island, although this theory is debated.

Another intriguing theory is the "walking" theory. Archaeologists experimented with this idea by creating a replica of a Moai and demonstrating that with ropes and manpower, the statue could be rocked forward in a walking motion. This theory suggests that the statues were transported upright in a way that mimicked walking, a process that would have required tremendous coordination and labor.

The purpose of the Moai is also a subject of debate. Most scholars agree that they were created to honor ancestors, chiefs, or other important figures. The statues likely played a significant role in the island's social and religious life, symbolizing the power and authority of the island's clans.

The story of the Easter Island statues is a testament to human ingenuity and creativity. The Moai remain a powerful symbol of the cultural heritage of the Rapa Nui people and offer a glimpse into a complex society capable of remarkable feats of engineering. The mystery of how these statues were moved and erected adds to their allure and continues to draw researchers and tourists alike to this remote island.

The Fate of the Roman Ninth Legion: A Legion Lost in Time

In the fabric of history, few tales are as intriguing and shadowy as the fate of the Roman Ninth Legion, a formidable force of the ancient world that seemingly vanished without a trace. The mystery of their disappearance is a puzzle set against the backdrop of the early 2nd century, a time when the Roman Empire was at the zenith of its power, yet faced constant challenges on its fringes. The Ninth Legion, renowned for their military prowess, entered the mists of Britain, and like a ghost, faded away, leaving behind a trail of legend and conjecture.

The story of the Ninth Legion, "Legio IX Hispana," is one woven from the threads of historical records and the fabric of myth. This legion, known for its bravery and discipline, was a key force in the Roman conquest of Britain, participating in significant battles and military campaigns. However, by the early 2nd century, records of the Ninth Legion began to dwindle, and then, abruptly, they disappeared from the annals of history.

Theories about their fate are as varied as they are fascinating. One of the most enduring claims is that the Ninth Legion met their end in Britain, possibly wiped out in a catastrophic battle against the indigenous tribes. This theory paints a picture of a valiant last stand, a Roman force overwhelmed by the fierce resistance of the Picts or other northern tribes. The lack of concrete evidence or a definitive battlefield only adds to the allure of this theory.

Another hypothesis suggests that the legion was transferred to another part of the Roman Empire, perhaps to the Rhine or Danube frontiers, or even to the East, and gradually disbanded or merged with other legions. This theory leans on the administrative and logistical nature of the Roman military, a less dramatic but plausible end to the Ninth Legion's story.

The mystery is compounded by the dearth of archaeological evidence. The last definitive record of the Ninth Legion's existence comes from the city of York, where they were stationed around AD 108. After that, the historical trail goes cold. No substantial remnants of the legion have been found, nor conclusive evidence of their destruction or reassignment.

The disappearance of the Roman Ninth Legion has inspired numerous tales and speculations. In literature and film, they have been immortalized as a symbol of the twilight of Roman Britain, a representation of the decline of Roman power in the face of relentless barbarian invasions. The Ninth Legion's story is emblematic of the uncertainties that lie at the heart of ancient history, where fact and legend intertwine inextricably, and is a tale that continues to captivate scholars, historians, and enthusiasts alike.

Graham Hodson

The Man in the Iron Mask: A Royal Secret of the Sun King's Reign

The Man in the Iron Mask is a tale that has captivated historians, novelists, and the public for centuries, enveloped in the mystery of his identity and the reason for his prolonged and secretive imprisonment. This enigmatic figure was a prisoner held during the reign of Louis XIV, the Sun King of France, in the late 17th century. His story is a blend of historical fact and imaginative speculation, a narrative that intertwines with the grandeur and intrigue of the French royal court.

The existence of this mysterious prisoner is not fiction. Historical records confirm that a man, whose face was perpetually hidden behind a mask, was held in various prisons, including the Bastille and the island fortress of Sainte-Marguerite. His identity was kept a strict secret by the direct order of King Louis XIV, leading to widespread curiosity both during and after his lifetime.

The earliest references to the masked prisoner appear in the writings of Voltaire, a French Enlightenment writer, who claimed the prisoner wore an iron mask and was treated with considerable respect by his jailers. Later, Alexandre Dumas popularized the story in his novel "The Vicomte of Bragelonne: Ten Years Later," part of the

D'Artagnan Romances, which included "The Three Musketeers." Dumas' portrayal of the prisoner as the twin brother of Louis XIV added a romantic and dramatic twist to the tale, fueling further speculation and myth.

Historical research, however, paints a slightly different picture. The man, whose existence is recorded in prison registers, was noted to have worn a black velvet mask, not iron, during his transportation and in public. He was arrested around 1669 and remained in custody under the supervision of the same jailer, Bénigne Dauvergne de Saint-Mars, for approximately 34 years until his death in 1703.

The identity of the Man in the Iron Mask has been the subject of numerous theories. Some historians have proposed he might have been a low-ranking noble involved in political intrigue or espionage. Others suggest he could have been an important diplomat or even a relative of the King. Among the more popular theories is that he was an illegitimate half-brother or even a twin of Louis XIV, hidden away to protect the legitimacy of the royal line.

Yet another theory posits that he might have been Eustache Dauger, a valet arrested for unknown reasons. This theory aligns with some historical accounts suggesting that the masked man's detention conditions were not overly harsh and befitting a servant rather than a high-ranking noble.

The true identity of the Man in the Iron Mask and the reason for his secretive and prolonged imprisonment remain unsolved. Despite various claims and hypotheses, no conclusive evidence has emerged to fully uncover the mystery of who he was and why he was condemned to a life behind a mask.

The masked prisoner's true identity, hidden behind the veil of history, remains one of the enduring mysteries of the age of Louis XIV.

The Beale Ciphers: The Cryptic Quest for Buried Treasure

Here we embark on the tale of the Beale Ciphers. These three encoded documents, supposedly written in the early 19th century, are said to reveal the location of an enormous treasure buried somewhere in the United States. The tale of the Beale Ciphers is a blend of history, mystery, and the allure of untold riches, engaging treasure hunters and cryptanalysts for over a century.

The story of the Beale Ciphers began in 1885 with the publication of a pamphlet titled "The Beale Papers," published by James B. Ward. The pamphlet narrates the story of Thomas J. Beale, who allegedly discovered a substantial cache of gold, silver, and jewels in the Rocky Mountains with a group of adventurers in 1819. According to the narrative, Beale and his party transported the treasure to Bedford County, Virginia, and buried it for safekeeping.

Fearing something might happen to him, Beale created three ciphers. The first cipher was said to describe the location of the treasure, the second cipher listed the contents of the treasure, and the third cipher supposedly revealed the names of Beale's associates and their next of kin. Beale then entrusted these ciphers in a locked iron box to a local innkeeper, Robert Morriss, in 1822, with instructions that they should be opened only if Beale or his party failed to return.

Years passed, and Beale did not return. Morriss, unable to solve the ciphers, eventually passed the documents to a friend. This friend, who remains anonymous in the pamphlet and is simply referred to as the pamphlet's author, claimed to have cracked the second cipher using a version of the United States Declaration of Independence as a key. This decoded message described the treasure as being worth over $63 million and included details of its contents. However, the other two ciphers, revealing the treasure's exact location and the heirs to whom it belonged, remained unsolved.

The publication of "The Beale Papers" ignited a treasure-hunting frenzy. Many skeptics believed the story was a hoax, possibly fabricated by Ward himself to profit from the pamphlet sales. However, the allure of a hidden treasure was too tempting for many to ignore. Amateur and professional treasure hunters flocked to Bedford County, excavating areas in the hope of uncovering Beale's treasure, but to no avail.

Over the years, cryptanalysts and codebreakers have attempted to solve the remaining Beale Ciphers. The challenge is daunting; without a key, similar to the Declaration of Independence used for the second cipher, decoding them is nearly impossible. Some experts have even questioned the authenticity of the entire story, noting inconsistencies and lack of historical evidence supporting Beale's existence or his treasure expedition.

The Beale Ciphers remain a captivating mystery, part history and part legend. Whether they are a complex hoax, a cryptographer's challenge, or indeed the key to a hidden treasure, they continue to intrigue and puzzle. The potential of untold riches buried underground fuels the ongoing quest to decipher these cryptic texts.

Graham Hodson

The Mary Celeste: A Maritime Mystery of the Atlantic

Few stories have sparked as much fascination and speculation as the mystery of the Mary Celeste. This American merchant brigantine, discovered adrift and deserted in the Atlantic Ocean in 1872, became the epitome of ghost ships and unexplained maritime phenomena. The fate of the Mary Celeste's crew remains one of the greatest enigmas of the sea, a story that combines elements of mystery, the unexplained, and the eerie nature of the ocean's vastness.

The Mary Celeste set sail on November 7, 1872, from New York City, headed for Genoa, Italy. Under the command of Captain Benjamin Briggs, the ship carried a cargo of industrial alcohol, a crew of eight, and the captain's wife and their two-year-old daughter. It was a routine voyage, expected to be uneventful, crossing the familiar waters of the Atlantic.

However, the Mary Celeste would never reach its destination. On December 5, 1872, the British brigantine Dei Gratia spotted the Mary Celeste adrift in the Atlantic, near the Azores Islands. Captain David Morehouse, acquainted with Captain Briggs, was surprised to see the vessel off course and in a disheveled state. He sent a boarding party to investigate, and what they found aboard the Mary Celeste has perplexed the world ever since.

The ship was in a seaworthy condition, with its cargo largely intact and undisturbed. The crew's personal belongings, the ship's papers, and navigational instruments were still there, except for the captain's logbook and a lifeboat, which were missing. The most alarming discovery, however, was the complete absence of the crew and the captain's family. The ship's only lifeboat was gone, and the last entry in the independent ship's log dated back to ten days prior, showing nothing unusual.

What had become of Captain Briggs, his family, and his crew? Numerous suppositions have been proposed to explain their disappearance from the Mary Celeste. One popular theory suggested that the crew, fearing an explosion due to the fumes from the alcohol cargo, abandoned ship and perished at sea. However, no evidence of a leak or fumes was found on board. Was it a mutiny, a pirate attack, or an insurance scam? Perhaps it was something more mysterious—an encounter with a maelstrom. But none of these theories held water; there was no sign of violence, no indication of foul play. Another theory proposed a waterspout or seaquake that frightened the crew into hastily leaving the ship.

Despite extensive investigations, including an official inquiry by the British Board of Trade, no conclusive evidence emerged to explain the crew's disappearance. Captain Morehouse and his crew, who salvaged the Mary

Celeste and brought her to Gibraltar, were exonerated of any wrongdoing.

Over the years, the Mary Celeste has inspired numerous fictional accounts, including a story by Sir Arthur Conan Doyle, which further embellished the mystery. The ship herself continued to sail under different owners before her deliberate wrecking off the coast of Haiti in 1885 as part of an attempted insurance fraud.

The disappearance of her crew remains unsolved, a haunting maritime riddle lost in the vastness of the Atlantic, a reminder of the sea's unfathomable mysteries and the enduring appeal of an unsolved story.

The Pioneer Anomaly: A Cosmic Puzzle Beyond Our Planet

Although this isn't officially an "unsolved" mystery, in the realm of space exploration, few phenomena have been as perplexing as the Pioneer Anomaly. This enigma involves the unexplained deviations in the trajectories of the Pioneer 10 and Pioneer 11 spacecraft, two of humanity's most distant and ambitious explorers. Launched in the early 1970s, these spacecraft were designed to venture out of our solar system, providing groundbreaking data about the outer planets and the limits of our cosmic neighborhood. However, as they journeyed into the depths of space, they began to exhibit small, inexplicable changes in their paths, a mystery that puzzled scientists for decades.

Pioneer 10 and Pioneer 11 were launched in 1972 and 1973, respectively, on missions to study the asteroid belt, Jupiter, Saturn, and the outer solar system. They were the first spacecraft to travel through the asteroid belt and make direct observations of the outer planets. After their primary missions were completed, both spacecraft continued on trajectories that would take them out of the solar system, a journey into the unknown.

The anomaly was first noticed in the early 1980s when navigational data from the Deep Space Network, which tracks and communicates with distant space missions, showed that both Pioneer spacecraft were not where they were expected to be. They were slightly closer to the Sun than predicted by their trajectories. This discrepancy was initially thought to be a minor curiosity, but as more data was collected, it became apparent that something unusual was occurring.

The spacecraft were experiencing a tiny, unexplained sunward acceleration, about 10^{-10} meters per second squared. This deviation, known as the Pioneer Anomaly, was extraordinarily small but consistent, and it was not accounted for by known forces such as gravitational attraction from the Sun or other celestial bodies, or by the pressure of solar radiation.

Numerous theories were proposed to explain the Pioneer Anomaly. Some scientists suggested the effect could be due to unseen dark matter in the solar system, or modifications to Newtonian gravity or general relativity. Others proposed more conventional explanations, such as gas leaks from the spacecraft or uneven thermal radiation.

In 2012, a comprehensive analysis by a team of scientists provided a more mundane but definitive explanation for the Pioneer Anomaly. Using data from both the Pioneer spacecraft and newly developed thermal models, the team concluded that the anomaly was caused by the anisotropic emission of thermal radiation. In simpler terms, heat generated by the electrical components inside the spacecraft and the radiation of this heat into space created a small but detectable force that gradually pushed the spacecraft slightly off-course.

This conclusion was supported by detailed analysis of the spacecrafts' design and the directionality of the heat emission. The study demonstrated that this small force, over the vast distances and timescales involved in the missions, was sufficient to cause the observed deviations in their trajectories.

The resolution of the Pioneer Anomaly is a testament to the persistence and ingenuity of scientists in unraveling mysteries of the cosmos. It highlights the complexities of space exploration and the intricate interplay of physical forces, even in the seemingly empty void of space.

Graham Hodson

The Hessdalen Lights: Norway's Luminous Enigma

In the remote valley of Hessdalen in central Norway, an extraordinary and unexplained phenomenon has captivated scientists, ufologists, and casual observers alike. Known as the Hessdalen Lights, these mysterious illuminations have been appearing in the sky with intriguing regularity since the early 1980s. The lights, varying in shape, intensity, and duration, have sparked numerous theories and investigations, yet their origin remains a captivating mystery.

The first widespread sightings of the Hessdalen Lights began in late 1981, with reports of strange lights floating or darting across the sky, often at great speeds. Residents in the small valley of Hessdalen, a sparsely populated area known for its rugged terrain and harsh weather conditions, were the first to notice these unexplained phenomena. The lights appeared in various colors, including white, yellow, red, and blue, and ranged from intense flashes to floating orbs that could last for over an hour.

The frequency of these sightings during the peak period in the early 1980s was astonishing, with lights observed 15 to 20 times per week, drawing attention from both national and international researchers and media. This influx of attention turned Hessdalen from a quiet, rural valley into a hotbed of scientific inquiry and curiosity.

Several research initiatives, notably Project Hessdalen, initiated by Dr. Erling Strand from the Østfold University College, have been established to study the phenomenon. Equipped with a range of scientific instruments, researchers have conducted extensive observations and measurements, attempting to unravel the mystery of the Hessdalen Lights.

Theories about the nature and cause of the lights are varied. Some scientists have proposed that the lights are the result of a complex interaction between metallic minerals in the valley and the sulfurous river running through Hessdalen. They suggest that this interaction could create a battery-like effect, generating electrical charges that manifest as light phenomena. Another theory posits that the lights could be a type of plasma, formed by the ionization of air and dust by alpha particles during radon decay.

Ufologists and enthusiasts of extraterrestrial phenomena have also taken an interest in the Hessdalen Lights, with some speculating that the lights could be evidence of alien activity or spacecraft. However, this theory is met with skepticism by the scientific community, which generally favors natural explanations.

Despite numerous studies and the collection of data, including photographic and radar recordings, the Hessdalen Lights remain an enigma. The phenomenon has decreased in frequency since the 1980s but continues to be observed intermittently, maintaining its allure as a scientific mystery.

The Hessdalen Lights phenomenon is not only a compelling scientific puzzle but also a source of cultural and tourist interest. The valley has become a destination for those eager to witness the lights, and it hosts a yearly scientific conference where researchers from around the world gather to share findings and theories.

The Placebo Effect: The Healing Power of the Mind

In the intricate world of medicine and healing, there exists a phenomenon as perplexing as it is powerful – the placebo effect. This effect, where patients experience real, therapeutic benefits from a fake treatment, has baffled scientists, doctors, and psychologists for decades. The story of the placebo effect is not just a tale of medical curiosity; it's a journey into the complexities of the human mind and its surprising influence on the body.

The term "placebo," Latin for "I shall please," was first used in a medical context in the 18th century. However, the recognition of the phenomenon dates back to ancient times, where healers often used inert treatments to appease patients. The modern understanding of the placebo effect began to take shape in the 20th century, particularly during World War II, when anesthesiologist Henry K. Beecher observed wounded soldiers requiring less pain medication than expected, likely due to the expectation of relief.

At its core, the placebo effect is a remarkable demonstration of the mind-body connection. When patients believe they are receiving an effective treatment, whether it's a pill, injection, or even a surgical procedure, they can experience genuine improvements in their condition. This effect has been observed in various medical scenarios, including pain relief, depression, anxiety, and even Parkinson's disease.

The power of the placebo effect lies in expectation and belief. When a person anticipates a positive outcome from a treatment, the brain can trigger a series of biochemical responses. For instance, in pain relief, the brain may release endorphins – natural painkillers – mimicking the effects of real medication. Similarly, the belief in a treatment's efficacy can trigger neurological pathways that affect mood and physical well-being.

The psychological basis of the placebo effect is also tied to the concept of conditioning. Just as Pavlov's dogs were conditioned to associate a bell with food, patients can associate medical interventions with health benefits. This conditioning can trigger a physical response, even when the treatment itself has no therapeutic value.

The placebo effect raises important ethical and practical questions in medical research and practice. In clinical trials, the placebo effect is a critical consideration, as it can influence the perceived effectiveness of actual drugs. To account for this, many clinical trials use placebo-controlled studies, where some participants receive a real treatment and others receive a placebo, without knowing which group they are in.

There is a famous story of a woman who had been diagnosed with terminal cancer and upon being told immediately started to lose weight, her hair fell out, she felt sick and had no energy. Eventually, she went into hospital to end her days in a private room with her family around. At the point where she was getting very close to the end, a doctor came into the room to say that they didn't know how it had happened, but they'd got her notes wrong and made other diagnostic and administrative mistakes and that she didn't have, and never did have, cancer. From the time of being told this, within three weeks the woman was fully well again and back home. She went from being seriously ill with her family in attendance to say their goodbyes to completely recovered, simply by the power of the mind and the placebo effect.

Despite its widespread recognition, the placebo effect is not universally effective and varies among individuals. Factors such as a person's expectations, the severity of the condition, and even cultural influences can affect the strength of the response. Furthermore, the effect is typically more robust in subjective symptoms, such as pain, than in objectively measurable conditions.

The story of the placebo effect is a fascinating exploration of the human psyche and its capacity to influence physical health. It challenges our traditional understanding of healing and underscores the importance of psychological and emotional factors in medical treatment. The placebo effect remains a powerful reminder of the intricate connections between mind and body, a testament to the idea that belief and expectation can, in and of themselves, be potent medicine.

Animal Mass Die-Offs: Nature's Unsettling Phenomenon

In the natural world, there are occurrences that not only mystify but also serve as stark reminders of the fragility and interconnectedness of life on Earth. Among these are animal mass die-offs, events where large numbers of a particular species suddenly die within a short period. These die-offs, occurring across various species and in different regions of the world, have puzzled scientists and raised concerns about the health of ecosystems. A notable instance is the mysterious and catastrophic die-offs of the Saiga antelope in Kazakhstan, which epitomizes this enigmatic phenomenon.

The Saiga antelope, a species that roams the steppes of Central Asia, has experienced several mass die-off events, the most devastating in recent memory occurring in 2015. In a span of just a few days, more than 200,000 of these antelopes, over half of the global population, perished in Kazakhstan. The suddenness and scale of this event sent shockwaves through the conservation community and prompted intense scientific investigations.

Initial observations of the die-off pointed to a complex interplay of factors rather than a single cause. The antelopes were found with symptoms suggesting a respiratory illness; however, the widespread nature of the event indicated an environmental trigger. Autopsies and analyses revealed the presence of a bacterium, Pasteurella multocida, typically harmless to the antelopes but which had turned deadly. The puzzle was to understand what had triggered this usually benign bacterium to become so lethal.

Research suggested a combination of environmental factors created a perfect storm for the bacteria to flourish. Unusually high humidity and temperature levels in the region may have played a role, altering the antelopes' immune systems and making them more susceptible to the bacteria. Additionally, changes in vegetation and the stress of calving season could have contributed to weakening the animals' resilience to infection.

The 2015 Saiga die-off is not an isolated incident. Mass die-offs have been recorded in various species around the globe, from starfish along the North American Pacific Coast to birds in Australia. These events often leave scientists grappling for explanations. Potential causes range from disease, environmental toxins, and climate change, to more direct human activities like pollution and habitat destruction.

Mass die-offs serve as indicators of broader environmental changes and can provide critical insights into ecosystem health. For instance, die-offs in marine life might signal changes in ocean temperatures or water quality, often tied to larger phenomena like climate change or pollution. In other cases, they can point to emerging diseases or imbalances in food webs.

The story of animal mass die-offs, including the tragic case of the Saiga antelope, is a compelling and troubling reminder of the vulnerabilities within natural systems. It highlights the urgent need for a deeper understanding of how environmental changes, whether natural or anthropogenic, impact wildlife. The phenomenon also underscores the need for effective conservation strategies to safeguard biodiversity and ecosystem resilience.

Graham Hodson

The Mothman: A Shadow in the Skies of West Virginia

Here we tell the tale of the Mothman, a mysterious creature sighted in the 1960s in Point Pleasant, West Virginia. This enigmatic being, described as a large, winged humanoid with piercing red eyes, has become a fixture of cryptozoological lore, inspiring fear, fascination, and a cult following. The story of the Mothman is a blend of eyewitness accounts, urban legend, and cultural phenomenon, a narrative that straddles the line between the unexplained and the improbable.

The Mothman saga began on November 12, 1966, in a cemetery near Clendenin, West Virginia. Five gravediggers working in the cemetery spotted something they described as a "brown human being" that flew over their heads, gliding from tree to tree. This strange sighting was the prelude to a series of bizarre events that would unfold over the next year in the Point Pleasant area.

The most famous encounter occurred on November 15, 1966. Two young couples, Roger and Linda Scarberry and Steve and Mary Mallette, were driving near an old World War II munitions site known as the "TNT area." They described encountering a large, white creature with glowing red eyes and large wings folded against its back. Terrified, they sped toward Point Pleasant to alert the police, claiming that the creature followed their car. Their story, when reported in the local newspaper, captured the community's imagination and fear, leading to an explosion of sightings and the birth of the Mothman legend.

Over the next year, more than 100 reported sightings of the Mothman were recorded. Descriptions varied, but common elements included a large, man-like figure with wings and red eyes. The sightings were often accompanied by strange phenomena, including unexplained lights in the sky and eerie television and phone interference.

The Mothman phenomenon reached its tragic apex on December 15, 1967, with the collapse of the Silver Bridge, which connected Point Pleasant to Ohio. The disaster, resulting from a structural failure, claimed 46 lives. In the wake of the tragedy, rumors swirled that the Mothman sightings and the bridge collapse were somehow connected, though no evidence supported this claim. Nevertheless, the association between the Mothman and the Silver Bridge disaster has become a staple of the legend.

Various theories have been proposed to explain the Mothman sightings. Some suggest that the creature was a large bird, such as a sandhill crane or an owl, misidentified under low light conditions. Others propose more paranormal explanations, including extraterrestrial beings and interdimensional visitors. The psychological phenomenon of mass hysteria has also been cited as a potential cause, with the initial sightings leading to a contagion of fear and subsequent misidentifications.

The Mothman legend has become deeply ingrained in the cultural fabric of Point Pleasant and beyond. The town hosts an annual Mothman Festival, attracting visitors from all over the world, and features a Mothman Museum and a statue of the creature. The story has also inspired books, documentaries, and a feature film, "The Mothman Prophecies," based on a 1975 book by John Keel.

Whether the Mothman is a misidentified animal, a paranormal entity, or a cultural creation, its story remains one of the most captivating unsolved mysteries of the 20th century, a shadowy figure that continues to hover in the twilight zone between reality and myth.

The Mysterious Death of Marilyn Monroe

Marilyn Monroe, an icon of beauty and glamour in the golden age of Hollywood, met an untimely and mysterious end in August 1962, an event that continues to fuel intrigue and speculation. Her death, ruled as a probable suicide, has been a subject of endless debate and conspiracy theories, intertwining Hollywood's glitz with a dark tale of mystery, fame, and speculation.

Marilyn Monroe, born Norma Jeane Mortenson, rose to fame in the 1950s, becoming one of the most popular and enduring sex symbols of her era. Her life was marked by both cinematic triumphs and personal struggles, including tumultuous relationships and battles with depression and substance abuse. Behind her glamorous public persona lay a troubled and vulnerable individual, grappling with the pressures of fame and personal demons.

On the morning of August 5, 1962, Monroe was found dead in her home in Brentwood, Los Angeles, by her housekeeper, Eunice Murray. The official cause of death was listed as acute barbiturate poisoning, with the Los Angeles County Coroner's Office ruling it as a probable suicide. Monroe was found lying nude on her bed, holding a telephone receiver in her hand, with empty bottles of pills that had been prescribed for her depression scattered around the room.

However, the circumstances surrounding her death have led to numerous theories and speculations. Questions about the timeline of her death, discrepancies in the witness testimonies, and the handling of the investigation have fueled doubts about the official ruling. Some theories suggest that Monroe was a victim of foul play, with various individuals and entities implicated, including high-profile figures in the entertainment industry, members of organized crime, and even political figures.

One of the most persistent theories involves Monroe's alleged relationships with President John F. Kennedy and his brother Robert Kennedy. Speculation suggests that her connections with the Kennedys and her purported knowledge of political secrets might have led to her being silenced. However, evidence supporting these claims is circumstantial and remains a matter of conjecture.

Others believe that Monroe's death was an accidental overdose, possibly a result of her chronic insomnia and reliance on prescription medication. Her mental health issues and the pressures she faced in her personal and professional life are often cited as factors that might have led to an unintentional overdose.

The death of Marilyn Monroe is a story that reflects the intersection of fame, tragedy, and mystery. It's a narrative that resonates with the fragility of human life beneath the veneer of stardom. Monroe's legacy as a cultural icon remains as powerful as ever, but her death continues to be shrouded in enigma, a tragic end to a luminous life that left behind more questions than answers.

In the tale of Marilyn Monroe's mysterious death, we find a blend of Hollywood's allure and the stark realities of life in the spotlight, a reminder of the eternal human fascination with beauty, tragedy, and the unknown. Her story endures as a poignant chapter in the history of American cinema and culture, a mixture of light and shadow, fame and solitude, forever capturing the imagination of those who look beyond the silver screen.

Graham Hodson

The Bell Witch: A Haunting Tale from Southern Folklore

Moving into the world of American folklore, few stories are as chilling as that of the Bell Witch, a sinister entity whose haunting of the Bell family in the early 19th century Tennessee has become a staple of Southern ghost stories. This tale, woven from the threads of unexplained phenomena, family tragedy, and eerie occurrences, continues to be a source of fascination and fear, a narrative that blurs the lines between reality and the supernatural.

The story unfolds in the rural community of Adams, Tennessee, where, in 1817, the Bell family began experiencing strange and inexplicable events. John Bell, the family patriarch, first encountered the haunting presence in the form of strange, gnawing sounds on the walls of their home. Soon, the phenomenon escalated into more alarming activities: the family heard chains dragging, gulping and choking sounds, and faint whispers that soon grew into distinct voices.

The epicenter of these disturbances was the youngest of the Bell children, Betsy. She suffered the most extreme torments, with accounts of her being slapped, pinched, and bruised by an invisible force. The entity that tormented the family became known as the "Bell Witch," though it was unlike any witch in conventional lore. It was a malevolent, unseen force capable of physical interactions, intelligent conversations, and even predicting the future.

As word of the haunting spread, the Bell Witch attracted the attention of curious neighbors and paranormal enthusiasts. The entity exhibited a wide range of behaviors; it could be playful and cordial one moment, then vengeful and violent the next. It reportedly held conversations with visitors, recited sermons from two churches simultaneously, and sang hymns in a chilling voice.

One of the most disturbing elements of the legend is the Bell Witch's supposed vendetta against John Bell. The entity frequently expressed its desire to kill him, leading to a prolonged period of suffering for Bell, who experienced episodes of facial twitching, difficulty swallowing, and a decline in health. In December 1820, John Bell died, and legend has it that the Bell Witch claimed responsibility, even interrupting his funeral with songs and laughter.

The haunting did not end with John Bell's death. The entity promised to return years later, and many believe it kept its word. Reports of strange phenomena in the area persisted, and the legend of the Bell Witch grew, becoming a staple of local folklore and a subject of fascination beyond Tennessee. Whether a product of mass hysteria, a genuine poltergeist, or an elaborate hoax, the legend of the Bell Witch continues to haunt the collective imagination.

The Chupacabra: The Bloodthirsty Cryptid of the Americas

In the world of cryptozoology, few creatures have captured the public's imagination quite like the Chupacabra. Its name, derived from the Spanish words "chupar" (to suck) and "cabra" (goat), means "goat-sucker." This legendary creature is infamous for its alleged attacks on livestock, particularly goats, leaving behind carcasses drained of blood. The Chupacabra has become a cultural phenomenon, especially in the Americas, where reports of sightings and attacks have been prevalent since the 1990s.

The story of the Chupacabra began in earnest in 1995 in Puerto Rico. Residents of the small town of Canóvanas reported losing livestock to a mysterious predator. The animals were found with puncture wounds, often in the neck, and reportedly drained of blood. The descriptions of the culprit varied, but the most common portrayal was of a creature standing about three to four feet tall, with leathery or scaly greenish-gray skin, sharp spines or quills running down its back, and glowing red eyes.

The Chupacabra quickly became a sensation, with news of the attacks spreading beyond Puerto Rico to many parts of the Americas, including Mexico, Chile, Brazil, and the United States. Each region had its own variation of the creature, with differences in size, color, and even the methods of killing prey. The widespread nature of these reports fueled speculation about the creature's origins and its ability to move between disparate geographic areas.

As the legend of the Chupacabra spread, various theories were proposed to explain its existence. Some believed it to be a previously undiscovered species, perhaps a type of wild dog or a more exotic creature. Others speculated about extraterrestrial origins, linking the Chupacabra to UFO sightings and alien abductions. There were also suggestions that it was the result of secret genetic experiments gone awry.

In their quest to unravel the mystery, scientists and skeptics approached the phenomenon from a more rational perspective. Many of the alleged Chupacabra carcasses that were examined turned out to be dogs, coyotes, or other canines afflicted with mange, a skin disease that causes hair loss and can give an animal a grotesque appearance. As for the livestock killings, wildlife experts often pointed to common predators like dogs or wild cats, noting that the supposed "blood-sucking" aspect of the attacks could be an illusion caused by the natural process of decomposition.

Whether as a misunderstood animal, a figment of collective imagination, or something more mysterious, the Chupacabra continues to be a topic of fascination and debate, a creature that dwells in the shadowy realm between reality and folklore.

Graham Hodson

The Tamam Shud Case: Australia's Most Enduring Mystery

On a serene summer morning in 1948, a perplexing mystery unfolded on the shores of Somerton Beach in Adelaide, Australia. This enigma, known as the Tamam Shud Case or the Mystery of the Somerton Man, revolves around an unidentified man found dead under baffling circumstances, a riddle wrapped in a cryptic note. The case remains one of Australia's most profound unsolved mysteries, combining elements of espionage, romance, and the unbreakable codes of silence from a bygone era.

On December 1, 1948, the body of an unidentified man was discovered lying against a seawall at Somerton Beach. Dressed in a suit and polished shoes, he looked more the part of a businessman than a beachgoer. The labels on his clothing were removed, and all personal identification was missing, leaving his identity a mystery. The autopsy revealed no obvious cause of death, though some signs suggested poisoning.

The intrigue deepened several months later when a small rolled-up piece of paper was found in a hidden pocket of the man's trousers. The paper bore the printed words "Tamam Shud," meaning "ended" or "finished" in Persian, a phrase found on the last page of a collection of poems called "The Rubaiyat" by Omar Khayyam. This clue led to the discovery of a particular copy of the book, which had been left in an unlocked car near the beach. In the back of the book, detectives found a phone number, an unidentified number, and a cryptic code, which has never been deciphered.

The phone number led to a woman named Jo Thomson, who lived near Somerton Beach. Although she denied knowing the deceased, witnesses later claimed they had seen a man resembling him in the vicinity of her house. During a police interview, Thomson appeared evasive and uncomfortable, leading to speculation about her possible connection to the man's death.

The cryptic code and the untraceable man gave rise to numerous theories: Was he a spy caught in the intricate web of Cold War espionage? Was it a case of unrequited love, linked to the enigmatic Jo Thomson? Or was it a more mundane explanation, a traveler who met an untimely end in a foreign land? Despite extensive investigations, no conclusive answers have been found.

Over the years, the Tamam Shud case has captivated detectives, historians, and cryptographers. Efforts to crack the code in the book and to identify the man using modern forensic techniques have so far yielded more questions than answers. The man's face, peaceful in death, has become an icon of mystery, a puzzle that beckons the curious and the investigative-minded.

Graham Hodson

The Authorship of Shakespeare's Works: The Bard's Enduring Enigma

In the world of literature, few names are as revered or as influential as William Shakespeare. The Bard of Avon, as he is affectionately known, is credited with penning some of the most celebrated plays and sonnets in the English language. However, for centuries, a debate has simmered over the true authorship of these works. The Shakespeare authorship question is a contentious and fascinating topic that combines literary analysis, history, and conspiracy theories, challenging our understanding of Elizabethan literature and the figure of Shakespeare himself.

William Shakespeare, a playwright and actor from Stratford-upon-Avon, England, is traditionally recognized as the author of 37 plays and 154 sonnets. His works, including renowned plays like "Hamlet," "Romeo and Juliet," and "Macbeth," have had an immeasurable impact on English literature and drama. However, since the late 18th century, some scholars and literary enthusiasts have questioned whether Shakespeare truly wrote these works.

The seeds of doubt were sown due to the scant historical record of Shakespeare's life, which some argue is insufficient to support his authorship. These skeptics point to Shakespeare's modest education, relatively humble origins, and the lack of contemporary documentation linking him directly to the works. Critics argue that the depth of knowledge displayed in the plays, particularly in areas such as law, philosophy, classical literature, and foreign languages, would have been unlikely for someone of Shakespeare's background.

As a result, alternative candidates have been proposed as the true authors of Shakespeare's works. These figures typically come from more privileged backgrounds with better-documented lives and, in some cases, known literary output. Some of the most prominent candidates include:

Sir Francis Bacon, a philosopher, scientist, and statesman, known for his intellectual prowess. Proponents of Bacon's authorship believe he may have sought anonymity to avoid the stigma of print, as the theater was considered a lower form of art during Elizabethan times.

Edward de Vere, the 17th Earl of Oxford, a nobleman and courtier with a known interest in theater and poetry. Supporters of the Oxfordian theory argue that his life and experiences closely mirror themes and events in Shakespeare's plays.

Christopher Marlowe, a contemporary playwright and poet. Some theorists suggest that Marlowe faked his early death in 1593 and continued to write under the pseudonym of William Shakespeare.

Despite these theories, the majority of Shakespearean scholars and literary historians support the traditional attribution to William Shakespeare of Stratford. They point to historical references and testimonies from Shakespeare's contemporaries that affirm his authorship. Moreover, they argue that the plays' understanding of human nature and society reflects a universal insight, not necessarily dependent on formal education or aristocratic experience.

The debate over the authorship of Shakespeare's works has transcended academic circles, capturing the public imagination and inspiring books, films, and theatrical productions. The question touches on broader themes of literary history, identity, and the nature of genius.

Regardless of one's stance on the authorship question, the enduring mystery adds another layer of intrigue to Shakespeare's works. Whether penned by the man from Stratford, a hidden noble, or another writer entirely, these works remain an integral part of the literary canon, a testament to the enduring power of storytelling and the enigmatic nature of artistic creation. The debate over the authorship of Shakespeare's works continues to be a captivating unsolved mystery, inviting each new generation to explore and speculate on the origins of some of the greatest works in the English language.

The Scream Painting Theft: A High-Stakes Art Heist and Recovery

The art world was shaken to its core one winter morning in 1994 when news broke of an audacious heist that seemed more akin to the plot of a Hollywood thriller than reality. Edvard Munch's iconic painting, "The Scream," had been stolen. This wasn't just a theft of high-value art; it was a brazen abduction of cultural heritage, an act that plucked one of the world's most famous and emotionally resonant paintings from its rightful place.

February 12, 1994, marked the start of the Winter Olympics in Lillehammer, Norway. While the world's attention was captivated by the spectacle of the games, thieves were orchestrating a heist of dramatic proportions. In the early hours, they broke into the National Gallery in Oslo. With remarkable audacity, they shattered a window, bypassed the building's minimal security measures, and lifted "The Scream" from the wall. To add insult to injury, they left a note reading "Thanks for the poor security," a mocking gesture that underscored the ease of their crime.

The theft of "The Scream" sent shockwaves through the international community. Edvard Munch's masterpiece, a symbol of existential angst and human anxiety, resonated deeply in the collective consciousness. Its absence was a cultural wound, leaving an empty space on the walls of the National Gallery and in the hearts of art lovers worldwide.

The Norwegian police launched a massive investigation, navigating a labyrinth of leads and dead ends. The public and the media speculated wildly - was this the work of a sophisticated criminal syndicate, or could it have been a stunt to draw attention to the Olympics? As days turned into weeks, hope of recovering the painting began to wane.

The breakthrough came when the police, working in conjunction with the British police and the Getty Museum, set a trap. In a sting operation that seemed as dramatic as the heist itself, they posed as art dealers and made contact with the thieves. After intense negotiations, a deal was struck for the return of the painting.

In a climax befitting a cinematic plot, "The Scream" was recovered in a hotel in Asgardstrand, Norway, in May 1994. The painting was largely undamaged, much to the relief of the art world. The police had outwitted the thieves and returned the painting to its rightful home, but questions lingered. Who were these thieves? What drove them to steal such a famous piece of art? Were they seeking ransom, or was it the thrill of stealing a national treasure?

The recovery of "The Scream" was celebrated globally, its return a testament to the perseverance of law enforcement and the international art community.

Graham Hodson

The Secret of Rennes-le-Château: A Tale of Hidden Treasures and Mysteries

Nestled in the hills of southern France lies the small, picturesque village of Rennes-le-Château, a place shrouded in mystery and intrigue. This seemingly quiet locale has been the center of an enduring enigma involving hidden treasures, secret societies, and controversial historical claims. The legend of Rennes-le-Château, a mix of history, myth, and speculation, has captivated treasure hunters, conspiracy theorists, and history buffs for decades.

The story of Rennes-le-Château's mystery began in the late 19th century with its parish priest, Bérenger Saunière. Saunière arrived in the village in 1885 and soon began extensive renovations of the church dedicated to Saint Mary Magdalene. It was during these renovations, according to local lore, that Saunière discovered something extraordinary, which led to a sudden and unexplained influx of wealth.

The nature of Saunière's discovery remains the subject of much speculation. Some believe that he found hidden documents or parchments, possibly linked to the Knights Templar or the Cathars, a medieval Christian sect. Others speculate that he might have uncovered a significant treasure, perhaps the legendary lost gold of the Visigoths or a hoard connected to Mary Magdalene, who, according to some legends, had fled to France after the crucifixion of Jesus Christ.

The mystery deepened with Saunière's lavish spending following his discovery. He renovated the church in an unusual style, incorporating symbols and statues that some interpret as coded messages. He also constructed a luxurious estate, including a tower named the Tour Magdala, which further fueled rumors about the source of his wealth.

The intrigue surrounding Saunière and Rennes-le-Château reached a wider audience in the 1950s and 1960s through books and articles that speculated about his findings. These works often linked the mystery to esoteric subjects, including the Holy Grail, the Ark of the Covenant, and secret societies like the Priory of Sion, a purported secret organization that supposedly protected the descendants of Jesus Christ and Mary Magdalene.

One of the most popular theories is that Saunière discovered proof of a bloodline stemming from Jesus Christ and Mary Magdalene, a theory popularized in the 1982 book "The Holy Blood and the Holy Grail" and later in the best-selling novel "The Da Vinci Code" by Dan Brown. This theory suggests that the knowledge of this bloodline was the true treasure of Rennes-le-Château, a secret guarded by the Priory of Sion and other historical figures.

Despite the intrigue, many historians and researchers dismiss the more sensational claims about Rennes-le-Château as modern myths and fabrications. They argue that the lack of credible historical evidence supporting these theories, coupled with the debunking of the Priory of Sion as a 20th-century hoax, casts doubt on the supposed mysteries linked to the village and its priest.

Nevertheless, the legend of Rennes-le-Château continues to be a topic of fascination and debate. The village has become a destination for those drawn to its mysterious past, eager to unravel the secrets that it may hold.

The Disappearance of the Amber Room: The Lost Treasure of the Tsars

In the mysterious world of lost treasures, few are as captivating and enigmatic as the Amber Room. Once considered the "Eighth Wonder of the World," this magnificent chamber adorned with amber panels, gold leaf, and mirrors was a masterpiece of baroque art. Its disappearance during World War II at the hands of Nazi Germany has given rise to one of the greatest mysteries of the modern era, a tale of war, plunder, and a relentless quest for a lost treasure.

The Amber Room began its journey in the early 18th century, initially installed in Charlottenburg Palace, home of Friedrich I, the first King of Prussia. In 1716, as a symbol of peace and shared admiration between Prussia and Russia, Friedrich Wilhelm I of Prussia gifted the room to Peter the Great of Russia. The Amber Room was then transported to Russia, where it was installed in the Winter Palace in Saint Petersburg and later moved to the Catherine Palace in Tsarskoye Selo.

Over the years, the room was expanded and embellished, eventually covering more than 55 square meters and containing over six tons of amber. The Amber Room was a marvel of its time, its panels intricately designed with gold leaf and mirrors, creating a dazzling effect that awed visitors.

The outbreak of World War II marked the beginning of the Amber Room's tragic fate. In 1941, with the Nazi invasion of the Soviet Union, the Amber Room fell into the hands of the invading forces. Despite attempts by the Soviets to conceal its panels behind mundane wallpaper, German soldiers dismantled the room within 36 hours, packing it into crates and transporting it to Königsberg (now Kaliningrad, Russia), where it was reinstalled in the city's castle museum.

The Amber Room's stay in Königsberg was short-lived. As the war turned against Germany, the city came under siege by the Red Army. In August 1944, Allied bombing raids severely damaged the city and its castle. After this point, the trail of the Amber Room goes cold. When Soviet forces took control of the city in 1945, the Amber Room was nowhere to be found.

The disappearance of the Amber Room has given rise to numerous theories and expeditions to locate it. Some speculate that it was destroyed during the bombing of Königsberg, its fragile amber panels incinerated in the fires that engulfed the city. Others believe that the panels were evacuated by the Nazis in the war's final days, hidden in a secure and undisclosed location.

Numerous searches have been conducted over the years in mines, caves, and beneath rubble in and around

Königsberg, but none have yielded the Amber Room. Treasure hunters, historians, and governments have all shown interest in recovering this lost masterpiece, but its whereabouts remain a mystery.

The Amber Room is not just a lost artifact; it represents the cultural losses suffered during war and the enduring impact of historical plunder. Its disappearance is a poignant reminder of the fragility and impermanence of art and beauty in the face of conflict.

Graham Hodson

The Princes in the Tower: A Royal Tragedy Shrouded in Mystery

A tale as old as time, yet as fresh as a wound unhealed, the mystery of the Princes in the Tower remains one of the most poignant and enduring puzzles in English history. It's a story woven from the threads of political intrigue, betrayal, and the innocence of youth caught in the ruthless machinations of power. The fate of Edward V of England and his younger brother Richard, Duke of York, is a narrative steeped in mystery, a tale of two young lives that vanished within the cold, formidable walls of the Tower of London.

The year was 1483, a time of upheaval and power struggles in England. The young King Edward V, a boy of 12, was en route to London for his coronation, escorted by his uncle, Richard, Duke of Gloucester. But upon arriving in the city, the course of events took a dark turn. The Duke had Edward and his younger brother Richard, merely 9 years old, lodged in the Tower of London, ostensibly for their protection until the coronation. However, the coronation would never take place.

In a stunning move, the Duke of Gloucester declared that the boys' father, Edward IV's marriage to their mother, Elizabeth Woodville, had been invalid, rendering the young princes illegitimate and ineligible for the throne.

The Duke then ascended the throne himself as King Richard III. The young princes, seen playing in the grounds of the Tower, slowly faded from public view, and whispers of their fate began to circulate.

The mystery deepened when, after the summer of 1483, the princes were no longer seen at all. What befell them within the Tower's ancient walls has been a subject of speculation and debate for centuries. Were they murdered to secure Richard III's claim to the throne? If so, who carried out the deed? Was it Richard III himself, as many have speculated, or were others involved in a more complex web of political intrigue?

Over the centuries, various accounts and rumors have surfaced. In 1674, during renovations at the Tower, the skeletons of two children were discovered in a chest buried beneath a staircase. Many believed these to be the remains of the lost princes, though conclusive identification has never been made.

The disappearance of the Princes in the Tower is a story that transcends the simple loss of two young lives. It is emblematic of the brutal nature of Medieval politics, where the ascent to the throne was often paved with treachery and bloodshed. It's a narrative that challenges historians and captivates the public imagination, a mystery that has inspired countless works of literature and art, most famously William Shakespeare's play "Richard III."

The fate of Edward V and his brother Richard remains one of history's great unsolved mysteries, a haunting question mark in the annals of England's past. It's a tale of innocence lost, a reminder of the fragility of life and the ruthless tides of power.

The Sea Peoples: The Enigmatic Raiders of the Bronze Age

One of the most enigmatic chapters of ancient history is the story of the Sea Peoples, a confederation of naval raiders who emerged during the late Bronze Age, around the 12th century BC. Their sudden appearance, ferocious attacks, and mysterious origins have puzzled historians and archaeologists for centuries. The Sea Peoples were instrumental in the Bronze Age collapse, a period marked by the decline and fall of several major civilizations in the Eastern Mediterranean and Near East.

The primary source of information about the Sea Peoples comes from ancient Egyptian records, particularly those of the pharaohs Merneptah and Ramesses III. These records depict a series of fierce conflicts between Egypt and the Sea Peoples, with detailed descriptions of battles and the names of different groups within this confederacy.

According to Egyptian inscriptions, the Sea Peoples embarked on a large-scale migration by sea and land, attacking and plundering cities along the coast of the Eastern Mediterranean. Their raids contributed to the destabilization and eventual fall of several powerful states, including the Hittite Empire, the Mycenaean kingdoms of Greece, and the city-states of the Levant.

The Egyptian texts name several groups among the Sea Peoples, including the Peleset (possibly the Philistines), the Denyen, the Shekelesh, the Tjeker, and the Weshesh. The origins of these groups are a matter of debate, with theories suggesting they may have come from different regions of the Mediterranean, such as the Aegean, Anatolia, the Balkans, or even the Italian peninsula.

The most significant encounters between Egypt and the Sea Peoples occurred during the reign of Pharaoh Ramesses III. In the eighth year of his reign, around 1178 BC, Ramesses III faced and repelled a massive Sea Peoples invasion by both land and sea. The Egyptians claimed a decisive victory, depicted in reliefs at Ramesses III's mortuary temple at Medinet Habu. These scenes provide valuable insights into the weapons, ships, and armor of the Sea Peoples.

Despite their impact on the ancient world, little is known about the political organization, culture, or language of the Sea Peoples. They did not leave written records, and the accounts of their enemies, primarily the Egyptians, are the primary sources of information, which may be biased or incomplete.

Several theories have been proposed regarding the origins and motivations of the Sea Peoples. Some suggest that they were displaced due to climatic changes, drought, or famine, leading them to migrate in search of new lands. Others hypothesize that they were part of a larger movement of peoples, possibly driven by economic or social upheaval in their homelands.

The Sea Peoples' raids and the broader Bronze Age collapse marked the end of an era in the ancient world. The destruction and instability brought by these events led to significant cultural and political changes, paving the way for the rise of new civilizations and the Iron Age.

Their sudden appearance, devastating impact, and subsequent disappearance from the historical record have left many questions unanswered.

Graham Hodson

The Disappearance of the Flannan Isles Lighthouse Keepers: A Lighthouse Shrouded in Mystery

The Disappearance of the Flannan Isles Lighthouse Keepers is a story wrapped in an enigma, a tale that has stirred the imagination and baffled experts for over a century. In December 1900, three lighthouse keepers vanished into thin air from the Flannan Isles Lighthouse, a lonely beacon perched on the edge of the world in Scotland's Outer Hebrides. Their names were Thomas Marshall, James Ducat, and Donald McArthur.

The mystery began when the steamer Hesperus, tasked with delivering supplies to the lighthouse, arrived on December 26, 1900, only to find a chilling scene. The lighthouse was eerily silent. No one responded to the ship's whistle or the fired rocket signals. Joseph Moore, a relief keeper, was sent ashore and discovered the main door closed, beds unmade, and the clock stopped. Strangely, the lamp was clean and refilled, ready to be lit.

As the investigation unfolded, more puzzling details emerged. The lighthouse logbook, usually a mundane record of daily activities, contained entries that were anything but ordinary. The entries, made by Marshall, spoke of severe storms and Ducat's quiet and McArthur's tearful demeanor, which was highly unusual for these seasoned keepers. However, the weather records on the mainland reported no such storms in the area at the time.

The final entry, dated December 15, read, "Storm ended, sea calm. God is over all." After that, nothing. The men had vanished without a trace, leaving behind a set of oilskin coats, one of which was missing, suggesting that one of the keepers had left the lighthouse in a hurry.

Several theories have been proposed over the years, ranging from the plausible to the fantastic. Some suggest that a freak wave swept the men away while they were securing the equipment outside. Others speculate about abduction by foreign spies, a dispute that led to murder-suicide, or even supernatural forces at play. But the true fate of Thomas Marshall, James Ducat, and Donald McArthur remains one of the greatest unsolved mysteries in maritime history.

This baffling disappearance invites us to ponder the limits of human understanding and the power of nature. It's a reminder that some secrets are kept by the sea, never to be revealed. The story of the Flannan Isles Lighthouse Keepers remains a haunting, unresolved whisper from the past, echoing through the corridors of time.

Take a look at more great books available from
Rockwood Publishing

... some for **FREE!**

Just visit the link below:

rockwoodpublishing.co.uk

to the subject matter covered. The information included in this book has been compiled to give an overview of the subject(s) and detail some of the symptoms, treatments etc. that are available to people with this condition. It is not intended to give medical advice. For a firm diagnosis of your condition, and for a treatment plan suitable for you, you should consult your doctor or consultant. The writer of this book and the publisher are not responsible for any damages or negative consequences following any of the treatments or methods highlighted in this book. Website links are for informational purposes and should not be seen as a personal endorsement; the same applies to the products detailed in this book. The reader should also be aware that although the web links included were correct at the time of writing, they may become out of date in the future.

Disclaimers

The content contained within this book is for information and entertainment purposes only, and in no way purports to represent professional medical opinion. It should NOT be used as a substitute for expert advice, and you must consult with your designated health professional before acting upon any information contained herein or before undertaking any practice whose methodology is referred to in this book. The author is NOT a registered health professional and the text merely represents personal opinion, not medical fact. The author cannot be held responsible for the consequences of any action derived from the reading of this book, as the content is not based on diagnosis and subsequent regimen. It is the reader's responsibility to seek proper, professional medical advice from a registered health practitioner in connection with any material contained within this book.

Legal Disclaimer (part 1)

Nothing in this book should be construed as an attempt to diagnose, treat or cure. The information in this book is intended to be a community resource. The author takes no responsibility for any informational material or brochures produced using information taken from this book. The author has endeavoured to ensure that all

information is correct at the time of publication. This information, however, is subject to change without notice. The author makes no warranty with regard to the accuracy of any information and will not be liable for any errors or omissions. Any liability that arises as a result of this information is hereby excluded to the fullest extent allowed by law.
This information should not be used as a substitute for seeking independent professional advice.

Legal Disclaimer (part 2)

Disclaimer and Terms of Use:

a) i. In publishing this information, the author makes no representations concerning the efficacy, appropriateness or suitability of any products or treatments. Use this information at your own risk. The compiler is not a doctor and has no medical background or training.

ii. Statements and information regarding dietary supplements, books and any products mentioned have not been evaluated by any health authority and are not intended to diagnose, treat, cure or prevent any disease or health condition.

b) In view of the possibility of human error, neither the author nor any other party involved in providing this information, warrant that the information contained therein is in every respect accurate or complete and they are not responsible nor liable for any errors or omissions that may be found or for the results obtained from the use of such information. The entire risk as to use of this information is assumed by the user.

c) You are encouraged to consult other sources and confirm the information.

d) The information you access is provided "as is". No warranty, expressed or implied, is given as to the accuracy, completeness or timeliness of any information herein, or for obtaining legal advice. To the fullest extent permissible pursuant to applicable law, neither the author nor any other parties who have been involved in the creation, preparation, printing, or delivering of this information assume responsibility for the completeness, accuracy, timeliness, errors or omissions of said information and assume no liability for any direct, incidental, consequential, indirect, or punitive damages as well as any circumstance for any complication, injuries, side effects or other medical accidents to person or property arising from or in connection with the use or reliance upon any information contained herein.

e) The author is not responsible for the contents of any linked site or any link contained in a linked site, or any changes or update to such sites. The inclusion of any link does not imply endorsement by the author. The author makes no representations or claims as to the quality, content and accuracy of the information, services, products, messages which may be provided by such resources, and specifically disclaims any warranties, including but not limited to implied or express warranties of merchantability or fitness for any particular usage, application or purpose.

f) The information provided is general in nature and is intended for educational and informational purposes only. It is not intended to replace or substitute the evaluation, judgment, diagnosis, and medical or preventative care of a physician, paediatrician, therapist and/or health care provider.

g) Any medical, nutritional, dietetic, therapeutic or other decisions, dosages, treatments or drug regimes should be made in consultation with a health care practitioner. Do not discontinue treatment or medication without first consulting your physician, clinician or therapist.

h) By reading this information, you signify your assent to these terms and conditions of use. If you do not agree to these terms and conditions of use, do not read/use this information. If any provision of these terms and conditions of use shall be determined to be unlawful, void or for any reason unenforceable, then that provision shall be deemed severable from this agreement and shall not affect the validity and enforceability of any remaining provisions.

i) The information, services, products, messages and other materials, individually and collectively, are provided with the understanding that the author is not engaged in rendering medical advice or recommendations.

j) The information and the terms of use are subject to change without notice. The material provided as is without warranty of any kind and may include inaccuracies and/or typographical errors. The author makes no representations about the suitability of this information for any purpose. The author disclaims all warranties with regard to this information, including all implied warranties, and in no event shall the author be held liable, resulting from, or in any way related to, the use of this information.

k) The unauthorized alteration of the content of this information is expressly prohibited. The author, its agents and representatives shall not be responsible for any claims, actions or damages which may arise on account of the unauthorized alteration of this information.